The Directors of the Orion Publishing Group
invite you to the 2006

Author Party

Thursday 16 February
The Great Gallery, The Wallace Collection
Manchester Square, London W1

6.00-8.00pm · Champagne

The Provost and Fel
invite you to Eton to celeb

esty the Queen's G
on

Thursday 9th May 200

Devon
ers Bal

cordially invi
y event in aid of
ember 2005 at

's Day
I have t

**We'll get on if
I'm in charge,
insists Harry**

rissa

TAMASIN'S
KITCHEN
CLASSICS
TAMASIN DAY-LEWIS

FOOD PHOTOGRAPHY BY **DAVID LOFTUS**   LOCATION PHOTOGRAPHY BY **ROBERT FAIRER**

WEIDENFELD & NICOLSON

CONTENTS

INTRODUCTION Last night I invented a pudding. A gingerbread and butter pudding seamed with sliced pears and strewn with jewels of stem ginger. I poured a home-made vanilla custard over it, made with rich Jersey milk, thickened with egg yolks and speckled with vanilla. I had been thinking of the ingredients for several weeks, imagining the taste, the texture, the detail: rich, voluptuous creaminess, grainy juiciness, spicy, damp treacliness. I was almost putting off the moment of reckoning in case it disappointed in any way, or I could come up with something better in the meantime. Perhaps, too, in a titillating sort of way, I had been waiting to get to the point where the imagined taste and expectation were at such fever pitch that there was only one thing for it – to go out, buy the ingredients and cook it.

Bread and butter pudding is one of those English classics that have endured. It may originally have come about as an inspired way of using up stale bread, old eggs and milk or cream that was on the turn, but that is how much of our classic cuisine was invented. Leftovers have always been the lifeblood of any good kitchen and serious cook. So now we make bread and butter pudding with brioche and panettone, with toasted teacakes, croissants or pain au chocolat. We spice it and scatter over vine fruits and dried apricots or prunes; we make it cheap with milk or lushly extravagant with Jersey cream. All are classics, all have their place and all, curiously, are as English as bread and butter pudding is in its original form, despite the introduction of Mediterranean or Middle Eastern ingredients.

It is the quality of the ingredients that is as crucial to a dish as the hand of a good cook; no amount of tinkering with inferior ingredients will produce a good result. And quality has been our strongest suit in Britain over the centuries: our beef, lamb and pork, sweet-cured bacon and hams; our fowl and game birds; our roots, summer vegetables and soft fruits; our orchards; our river fish, shellfish and cold-water fish; our milk, cream, eggs, hens and wonderful British cheeses.

We have been criticised for centuries for our plain or plain awful cuisine, but the truth has never been told forcibly and proudly enough: if you rear, grow and produce the best, what need have you to cover up and conceal; sauce and enrich; spice and sugar and complicate? Classic English food is good precisely because it is unmasked, unfussed with. It tells a simple tale and it tells of provenance and seasonality.

We may have blurred the seasons and imported more exotica in the last two decades than at any time in our considerable culinary history, but the essence of our classic dishes – without any modish twists of lemongrass or pinches of star anise, froths of truffle jus or squeezy bottles of herbed oil – is in our everyday roasting, baking, braising and grilling. It is in the marriage between a well-hung grouse stuffed with late summer raspberries, or a slow-reared hen smothered in tarragon butter and slow roasted in the oven; in a Middle White pork chop, with a snowy ribbon of white fat and rind, grilled with buttery apples and a splosh of Somerset Cider Brandy; in a purple pile of Dorset 'Herbert' blueberries turned in cinnamon sugar and baked into fluffy muffins.

Our greatest dishes don't rely only on ingredients grown on our land or fished from our shores. We would not manage without Sicilian lemons and Seville oranges; without the exotic fruits we crave in the winter, or the oils, vegetables and cheeses we buy from Italy, France and Spain. We need foreign spices and rices; pastas, polentas and pulses; sticky, dried vine fruits and stoned fruits; vinegars and nut oils; fungi and wine. We enhance, we borrow and we copy. We adapt, we improvise and we steal. All cooks in all kitchens have done so since the first fire was lit and the first meats and cereals transmogrified into roasts and breads. Our classic dishes are constantly evolving, particularly now we live in an age when a more global cuisine has replaced small-scale regionality.

I have no creed or credentials when it comes to defining the classics, other than a sense of what I have been eating and how my food and cooking has changed and evolved over the last four decades since I was a child. You might, therefore, feel cheated if you were hoping for a book that ventured no further than ye olde English baron of beef, steak and kidney pud, devilled kidneys and poached salmon; a book that strayed only onto accepted foreign terrain of l'ancien variety: coq au vin, blanquette de veau and duck a l'orange.

This is not that book. This is a book full of the recipes that have become MY classics, however recently. They may have originated in a well-known form, like the bread and butter pudding, but my tinkering has turned them into something where classic techniques and ingredients are only the starting point; the aim is to go beyond.

Do you remember Robert Carrier's *Great Dishes of the World*? It was a classic of its time, but one which melted the pot and opened our eyes to the flavours we had never dared play with and knew little about. It made us experiment, broadened our horizons. We didn't lose our identity so much as question the parameters of the one we had and push the boundaries a little.

Elizabeth David did the same for us with her vibrant prose and exploration of the warmer zones beyond our shores. The pull of the Mediterranean, with its sun-warmed fruits and vines, its plump-fleshed, heat-drenched vegetables, and olives, herbs and honey, is a land from whence we have never returned since she first drew its picture and tempted us with its scents and smells and recipes. Claudia Roden has done the same with her writing on the Middle East, and Anna Del Conte with her comprehensive gastronomical tour of Italy and its greatest of regional cuisines.

Perhaps we have borrowed more than any other country in the past, and continue to do so now in an era when our chefs are forever in search of the newest and most original shape, form, taste and texture, of scientifically researched combinations to set on our plates and set our palates afire. Yet I can't help feeling that our borrowing can be both our undoing and our inspiration; it always all comes down to the pair of hands cooking the dinner, and the palate, taste and imagination of the cook.

It is just as original, to my mind, to cook a perfect sirloin of Longhorn beef as it is to amaze with a work of cheffy culinary art, which the average home cook would never be able to accomplish. Think of steamed redcurrant curd pudding, a mellow plum and whiskied brown Betty, or a dried fig, hazelnut and walnut treacle tart. These are the sorts of dishes that take the word classic to heart and serve it with a twist, a sharp spike of revitalisation.

I like to think my kitchen classics are things of comfort and refinement; of simple elegance and sustenance. They fit like a pair of old slippers or a couture dress; they are about taste not money, and, while they should be pleasing to behold, they are neither tricksy nor over-decorated.

The most complicated confections are rarely the things you feast your eye upon with the kind of unbridled greed and desire you feel for your kitchen classics. A classic dish is something that will enter the annals of your family life and become part of its very fabric. It will be remembered and demanded, looked forward to and back upon, and you will go on delighting in making it for those you love best. You won't serve it too often either, or it will lose currency; it has to have rarity value, has to feel special, has to be something you keep nearly but not quite unattainable.

All but a tiny handful of these recipes are new, even if they are dishes I've been refining and tinkering with throughout my cooking life. Some are so new I cooked them for the first time when we shot the photographs for this book. However, they are all dependent on techniques or other similar dishes I have cooked over the years. What I hope is that you will find a treasure trove of recipes within these covers and that they may become the contemporary classics of your own kitchen as they have of mine; the best-loved dishes that your friends and family enjoy; dishes you can cook to perfection on autopilot and will evolve as you tinker with them yourself.

Early morning post-run hit of chestnut honey with hot water. My restorative. Is there anything honey doesn't cure and soothe?

A CLASSIC START

1

HOT BACON AND EGG SALAD

SERVES 4

2 heads of chicory (white or Treviso)
heart of a cos lettuce
freshly ground black pepper
4 rashers organic smoked streaky bacon, rinds
  removed (I use Swaddles which has no nitrites)

good white and red wine vinegar
4 large organic eggs
2 thick slices of sourdough bread, crusts cut off
1 clove of garlic and a little olive oil
1 tbsp snipped chives

Put the washed chicory and salad leaves in a large salad bowl and scrunch over some black pepper. Start cooking the bacon rashers in a small frying pan with no added fat. You want to keep frying beyond the point where the fat has started running and allow the bacon to brown and crisp on both sides.

While the bacon is frying, half fill another frying pan with water that you have acidulated with a few tablespoons of white wine vinegar. Bring the water to the boil and then turn it down to a gentle simmer. Break the eggs into a ramekin, one at a time, and gently drop them into the water. Cook until the whites have set, but the yolks are still soft. I shoosh hot water over them gently as they cook until the yolks have a translucent veil. Remove with a flat, slotted spoon to a plate. You can always return the eggs to the simmering water for 30 seconds if they have cooled down or you have cooked them a little too soon.

Rub the bread with a cut clove of garlic, brush with a little olive oil and cut into croutons. Bake the croutons in a hot oven briefly until they are crisp on both sides but not too browned. When the rashers are crisp, pour the hot bacon fat on to the salad leaves and break the rashers over the top; they should shatter like glass if they are crisp enough. Heat three tablespoons of red wine vinegar and let it bubble and reduce a little while you lay the eggs across the leaves and scatter over the croutons. Pour on the reduced vinegar, add the finely snipped chives over the salad and serve. I think salt is unnecessary as the bacon is quite salt enough.

Sometimes, just occasionally, I come up with an idea for a dish that speaks to the heart. A dish that has been inspired by the ingredients and style of a place, bears its imprimatur, pays homage, without my feeling the slightest sense of plagiarising or lack of authenticity. When I come back from a food trip or holiday my head is full of ideas, but I have to get to work fast, sensing that what I've absorbed about a place and its cuisine has to be translated quickly, before the immediacy of the memory fades.

After an intense few days of eating and discovering in Lyon with Rob at the end of this January, seeking out the buchons and multiple-starred restaurants of Lyon and Roannne – Bocuse, Têtedoie, Troisgros – I was sated with the richly meaty classics, the bacon fat, the pommes de terres sautées à la lyonnaise, the Burgundy. I came home and made

a salad. The kind of salad that, unusually, was also something of a comfort blanket – substantial, warm, filling, yolky and yet sharp, crisp, salt and soft all in one go, and as suitable for a brunch or late breakfast as for a late lunch, starter or light supper. This is it. When we cooked it for the photograph on the previous page, we all fell upon it afterwards, the sticky, crocus-coloured yolks still with a memory of warmth to them, the bacon crisped to snapping point, the reduced vinegar adding a note of sharpness to the gorgeous fat of the rashers. I baked the croutons in the oven – that way they weren't leaking oil like a tanker, and oil is the thing here, not butter.

The influence is obvious if you know Lyon – they cook a lot of pork and use bacon fat. And Michel Troisgros, the third generation of the eponymous three star, has become known for his delicate acidulation of even the richest of dishes. If you are making this for lunch or supper rather than as a starter, use two eggs each and an extra rasher. How could something so simple be so delicious? Just try it and see if you don't agree.

SMOKED PAPRIKA ROES ON TOAST

SERVES 2

seasoned flour for coating
225g/8oz herring roes
a pinch of Spanish smoked paprika (piccante
  pimentón)
30g/1oz unsalted butter
55g/2oz softened unsalted butter for the toast

2–4 slices sourdough bread, toasted and crusts
  removed
lemon juice
sea salt and black pepper

Pour a handful of flour and some sea salt and black pepper into a ziploc bag, add the roes and shake until they are coated. Put the floured roes onto a plate and sprinkle a pinch of smoked paprika along the length of each roe.

Melt the butter in a frying pan. When it begins to bubble, add the roes, paprika side down, and scrunch over some more black pepper. While they are frying, make and butter the toasts and put them on the plates. After a couple of minutes or so, add a pinch more paprika to the tops of the roes just before you turn them, when they have begun to crispen. Cook for another few minutes until they are firm.

Turn the roes onto the toasts and squeeze a little lemon over the tops, adding a little sea salt at the same time.

There used to be two tea shops in Petersfield when I was at school nearby. Every Wednesday afternoon we'd walk across into town and agonise over which it was to be: The Donkey Cart's soft roes on toast or The Punch and Judy's chocolate fudge cake? If we had enough pocket money we'd do both; there's nothing as greedy as a hungry teenager.

Herring roes, like herrings, are never on menus these days and never, in my experience, served when you go to lunch or supper with friends. It must have something to do with their status as poor man's food. On the west coast of Ireland, in County Mayo, people used to be known as 'herring chokers', a term of abuse, or at least disdain, for those known not to be able to afford beef or serious victuals.

This recipe and the following one make lovely starters or light lunch or supper dishes, or you could serve them as a savoury, daringly retro but well due for a comeback or at least a surprise if you're not serving pudding. Herring roes are a seasonal thing; the female herring is plump with them in May, but they are available all the year round frozen.

SOFT ROES ON TOAST WITH CAPER AND SHALLOT BUTTER

SERVES 2

seasoned flour for coating
225g/8oz herring roes
1 tsp finely minced shallots
1–2 tsp capers, desalinated and chopped
55g/2oz softened unsalted butter for the toast

2 lemons
sea salt and black pepper
2 or 4 slices of sourdough bread toasted, crusts
  removed
30g/1oz unsalted butter for cooking

Pour a handful of flour and some sea salt and black pepper into a ziploc bag, add the roes and shake until they are coated. Put the floured roes onto a plate, shaking off any excess flour, then work quickly so the flour doesn't begin to clog.

Mash the shallots and capers into the softened butter with a fork and add a spritz of lemon juice and some seasoning. Spread it thickly over the pieces of toast.

Melt the 30g/1oz of butter in a frying pan and when it begins to bubble throw in the roes. Fry for 2–3 minutes until the roes begin to look firmed up to about half their thickness, then turn them making sure you don't break them up. Fry the other side until it begins to brown. They should take 4–5 minutes altogether. Pile the roes on the spread toasts and put quarters of lemon alongside to squeeze on top.

TARTARE OF TUNA WITH CHICORY

MAKES 24

6 heads of chicory
285g/10oz fresh tuna steak
2 tsp finely chopped shallots
1 tsp finely chopped garlic

1 tsp finely chopped ginger
1 tbsp finely snipped chives
½ tsp crushed black peppercorns
1 tbsp Japanese soy sauce

Trim the bases of the chicory and carefully pull off the outer leaves, saving the hearts for a salad. Lay 24 of the leaves on a flat plate or tray, like little boats.

Slice the tuna as thinly as you can, then slice it again into strips. Chop the strips into little dice, then chop again until you have a really fine texture. Food processors are out – the result would be a minced mulch.

Mix the tuna well with all the other ingredients. Using two teaspoons, mould small amounts of the mixture into little quenelles and place one on each chicory leaf. Cover with clingfilm and chill if you are not going to eat them immediately.

I'm not a great one for the horrors of small food, even the word canapé reduces me to a state of near rebellion. These are the things that a full complement of chefs in a kitchen can perform but not a home entertainer, struggling to cook a good dinner for friends after a day's work. There are no greater stimulants to the appetite than salt and chilli, so a few hunky shards of best Parmesan or some smoke-roasted, salted almonds are perfectly good enough to prime your guests' palates for the things ahead. These delicious morsels, however, are not all about fiddling and twiddling, and they provide the necessary hot, salt hit that pre-dinner drinks are really all about.

As for these pretty, delicious, raw mouthfuls, I first came across them a couple of years ago in one of Rowley Leigh's columns, and knew that they must be good.

SMOKED HADDOCK RAREBIT WITH TOMATO VINAIGRETTE

SERVES 4

450g/1lb or so piece of thickly cut natural smoked haddock
150ml/5fl oz milk for cooking the haddock
a bay leaf
300ml/10fl oz thick béchamel (see page 196)
1 tsp English mustard powder or a heaped tsp grain mustard
Worcestershire sauce, Tabasco and Guinness (all optional)

110g/4oz mature unpasteurised Cheddar like Montgomery, Quicke's or similar, grated
2 egg yolks (optional)
4 tomatoes, skinned, cored and sliced
a little vinaigrette dressing
1 tbsp chopped chives
sea salt and black pepper
4 tbsp freshly grated Parmesan

Poach the haddock for 10–15 minutes in the milk with the bay leaf. Leave the fish to cool to warm, before gently pulling away the skin. Divide into four pieces.

Make the béchamel sauce (see page 196), a little thicker than usual, or use some you have already made. Warm it gently and while the pan is on the heat, add the mustard and any of the optional ingredients you fancy, then the grated cheese. Remove the pan from the heat the moment you have the strength of cheesy flavour you like and the cheese has melted into the sauce. Whisk in the egg yolks off the heat if you are using them. Check the seasoning.

On each plate put a single layer of tomato slices in two rows, spoon on a little dressing and add some chopped chives. Put a piece of fish on top. Pour enough sauce over each piece of fish to cover it and sprinkle over the Parmesan. Put the plates on the grill pan and blast right under the flame until the top is bubbling and brown.

Traditionally, this has always been made with British hard cheeses: Cheddar, Lancashire or Cheshire. The simple way of cooking it is just to slap the slices of cheese on bread and melt them under a hot grill until bubbling, but this does produce a somewhat oily, one-dimensional result. Adding English mustard powder or grain mustard, melting the cheese into a good, extra-thick béchamel, adding Tabasco, a couple of tablespoons of Guinness and a brace of egg yolks, all offer a degree of refinement that lifts this dish from the mundane to the marvellous. Better still, cloak a piece of smoky poached haddock with the sauce and a grating of best Parmesan and blast it quickly until the top is burnished and bubbling. Underneath the fish, put a layer of skinned tomatoes dressed with vinaigrette speckled with chives, and you have a dish to dine on or a great start to a supper.

COQUILLES ST JACQUES

SERVES 4

8 large scallops

300ml/10fl oz béchamel sauce of which 60ml/2fl oz should be double cream

1 tbsp breadcrumbs

1 tbsp freshly grated Parmesan

mashed potato made with about 340g/12oz of potatoes, milk, butter and seasoning

For the duxelles

2 shallots, finely chopped

30g/1oz unsalted butter

110g/4oz button mushrooms, thinly sliced

sea salt and black pepper

100ml/3½fl oz dry white wine

a sprig of thyme and a little lemon juice

To prepare the scallops, separate the corals and halve the white discs around their circumference, gently removing all the sinewy bits.

Make the béchamel (see page 196) and keep it warm while you cook the duxelles. First, sauté the shallots gently in the butter until golden and softened. Throw in the finely sliced mushrooms and cook them down until their juices have started to run. Season, add the wine and thyme and bring to the boil. Simmer until the wine has virtually disappeared. Take the pan off the heat, remove the thyme and squeeze in a little lemon juice.

Divide the mixture between four scallop shells. Put the scallop discs over the duxelles with two commas of coral to each portion.

Spoon some warm béchamel over each shell and sprinkle over the breadcrumbs and most of the Parmesan. Let the dish cool and set in the fridge for 30 minutes.

Preheat the oven to 200°C/400°F/gas 6. Spoon the mashed potato over the filling or around the edge of the shell and sprinkle over the last of the Parmesan. Bake for 20 minutes. Then put the shells under a hot grill to give them a final burnish before serving.

This wonderful classic Parisian dish, not to be confused with the Provençal version, is really fish pie served in the shell. Piping potato, as they would in any French bistro or brasserie serving St Jacques, is something I can't quite bring myself to do. I feel that should be left to the restaurants, while the home cook should just burnish the creamy mash under the grill and be done with it.

I suspect many of the best recipes since time began have been the result of mistakes or empty fridge syndrome. This was one of them, though it doesn't quite fall into either category. I had brought a huge crab back from the fishmonger to turn into a crab salad. When I got to work with the hammer and bashed the crab open, it was empty but for about 110g/4oz meat. My plan totally scuppered, what to do? I had cream, Parmesan, Oloroso sherry, cayenne, eggs. I threw everything into the blender with the crab and a hit of Dijon (great in a crab tart), then poured the velvet-smooth custard into ramekins to steam slowly in a bain-marie in the oven. The result? Untold richness and deliciousness, a thing of wonder and amazement, less a sow's ear than a silken, smooth custard that tasted as though it was one of life's more difficult concoctions to create. Not so, try these and see what you think. I think they are best eaten warm, with a lovely tremble to their middles. They keep well enough in the fridge to eat cold or warmed up if you make too many, but the first day is the best.

LITTLE CRAB CUSTARDS

SERVES 6

225g/8oz fresh crabmeat, brown and white
4 organic eggs, beaten
450ml/16fl oz double cream, Jersey if you can get it
2 dsrtsp Oloroso or Fino sherry

2 tsp Dijon mustard
knife tip of cayenne
2 tbsp freshly grated Parmesan
sea salt

Preheat the oven to 180°C/350°F/gas 4. Simply put all the ingredients into a liquidiser and blitz. Taste for seasoning, remembering that you need warmth, not heat, a sense of mustard, Parmesan and sherry, but none more pervasive than the others.

Place six ramekins in a roasting tin and pour the crab mixture into them. Put a layer of greaseproof paper over the top to stop a skin from forming on the custards. Pour boiling water into the roasting tin to come halfway up the sides of the ramekins. Cook for 25–30 minutes or until just set and with a tremulous centre. Remove the custards from their watery bath to a rack and serve when warm, with either a small salad or some good granary toast.

MACKEREL RILLETTES

SERVES 4–6

enough salt to cover the fish fillets
1 organic lemon
1 organic lime
1 dsrtsp coriander seeds, ground in a mortar
750g/1lb 10oz mackerel, filleted (a good
  fishmonger will do this for you)

sherry vinegar
1 clove of garlic
2 tbsp olive oil
3/4 tsp chilli flakes or finely diced dried chilli
15 basil leaves
cracked black pepper and sea salt

Place the salt in a bowl and finely grate the lemon and lime zest over it. Add the ground coriander and mix. Spread some of the aromatic salt to a depth of 2mm on a flat plate, then press the mackerel fillets into it, skin side down. Sprinkle with a little sherry vinegar and add more salt so that the fillets are completely covered. You can do this in two layers if your plate isn't big enough to do it in one. Leave for 45 minutes.

Meanwhile, peel the garlic and press it with the flat of a knife to crush it. Remove the green germ from the middle. Put the garlic, olive oil and chilli in a small pan and warm over a low heat for 10 minutes. Do not let the garlic brown and burn or the oil will become bitter. Remove the pan from the heat and set aside. Once it is cool, strain the oil through a sieve.

When the fish is ready, wash it thoroughly to remove all the salt, then remove the skin with a sharp knife. Place the fish in a bowl and add the flavoured oil. Using a fork, mix well, shredding the flesh as you go. Finely chop the basil and add it to the fish. Cover and place in the fridge for at least a couple of hours.

To serve, place little mounds of fish on small plates and sprinkle over some sea salt and freshly ground pepper. Have some fingers of granary toast or good warmed bread on the side.

Here is Heston Blumenthal's way with mackerel and a very good way it is too. This is a dish you can prepare ahead, at least three hours before you want it, but it will sit tight in the fridge for a couple of days if you need it to. I am spoilt by the wild waters of the west coast of Ireland in the summer, where the dolphins swim into the bays off the Atlantic coast of Mayo hunting mackerel. My neighbours bring round freshly caught, petrolly striped fish as taut as the line they were caught on, their sleek, silver underbellies plumped, firm and sticky. There is no mackerel like a fresh mackerel – their oil turns quicker than any fish I know – so we gut and bubble them under the grill almost as fast as you can say Holy Mackerel. The rest of the year I buy mackerel from my fishmonger and prefer to use them in ceviches or tartares – the hot spice and sharpness enhance the oily flesh.

There's not much you can do to make raw mackerel cut the mustard, visually speaking. This is a taste it and see dish.

This is a lovely plain winter salad, which you can make with white chicory and red Treviso chicory together if you like. You may dress it up with slices of orange and a little of the juice mixed into the dressing, or add some crunch with salted, buttered walnuts caramelised in a goo of maple syrup. Or leave well alone and eat it plain. This sort of salad cuts oily fish like mackerel and herring very well, or complements meats like duck or goose.

CHICORY SALAD

SERVES 4

6 heads of white chicory or mixed white and red Treviso chicory
2 tsp grain mustard
2 tbsp aged balsamic or sherry vinegar
8–10 tbsp cold-pressed olive oil, a good peppery one like Ravida or Nuñez de Prada
sea salt and black pepper
30g/1oz unsalted butter
a handful of whole shelled walnuts
1 tbsp maple syrup
1–2 tbsp chopped chives

Chop the chicory into a combination of stubby circles and leaves. Mix the mustard, vinegar, olive oil and seasoning to make the dressing to your taste. I like a lot of mustard to coat the leaves.

Heat the butter in a small frying pan. When it begins to bubble, throw in the walnuts and immediately shake over a little salt. Turn the walnuts in the butter for a couple of minutes before adding the maple syrup. It will splutter and bubble, but keep stirring to amalgamate it with the buttery nuts. Remove from the heat after a couple of minutes when the mixture is still a little liquid. Dress the salad, throw over the hot nuts and toss with the chives before serving.

Make this with chicken livers if you like, but it is a treat to find the richer, denser duck livers, the flavour of which is such a foil to the grapes. The discovery of pomegranate molasses, so much a part of Middle Eastern and Moroccan cooking, is a revelation when you want a complex, lemony underscoring without the acidity of the lemon itself. Make sure you buy really good brioche from a proper bakery, not supermarket pappy ones that always seem to leave a back-taste of synthetic vanilla and don't have that lovely eggy brightness and texture that you can pull apart.

DUCK LIVER WITH GRAPES

SERVES 4

340g/12oz duck livers, any green patches or tubey bits removed

sea salt, black pepper, cayenne

a little flour

30g/1oz unsalted butter

2 brioches, topknots removed, cut into thick slices

90ml/3fl oz duck or chicken stock (see page 194)

3 tbsp Madeira or Marsala

2 dozen Muscat grapes, peeled, halved and pipped

1–2 tsp pomegranate molasses

Season the livers with salt, pepper and a knife tip of cayenne. Roll them in a dusting of flour, shaking off the excess – you want just enough to help them crisp delectably. Melt the butter in a small pan and when it is foaming put in the livers. Turn them after a couple of minutes and cook the other side for another few minutes. They will take about 5 minutes to cook to crisped exteriors and meltingly pink middles. Remove to a warm plate.

Toast the brioche slices on a griddle or in a toaster and keep them warm. Deglaze the pan with the stock and booze, scraping as you go. Throw in the grapes, just to heat through with the pomegranate molasses. Taste after you have added the first teaspoon of molasses to see if you want to go farther. It mustn't overwhelm. Season, then remove the grapes with a slotted spoon and let the juices reduce. Meanwhile, put the livers on top of the brioche slices, pile on the grapes and pour the sticky pan juices over the lot. A little more butter added at the juice reduction stage, just a walnut-sized piece, gives extra gloss and butteriness.

PARMESAN CHEESE STRAWS

MAKES A GREAT PILE
450g/1lb sheet puff pastry, chilled

up to 225g/8oz best Parmesan, grated
on a medium grater

Preheat the oven to 220°C/425°F/gas 7. Scatter half the Parmesan on a marble slab or pastry board and set your pastry down on top. Roll the pastry and, before it is fully rolled, scatter the remaining Parmesan over the top, rolling it into the pastry as you go.

Cut the pastry into thin strips. Twist each strip as you would a rope, holding either end as you do and making a wavy rope shape. Place on a silicone or greaseproof sheet on a baking tray – no butter needed as the pastry is quite greasy enough.

Bake in the oven until gloriously golden along their whole length. If there are anaemic patches the pastry won't be cooked right the way through. The straws take 10–15 minutes to bake in my oven, but keep checking. Cool on a rack and serve while still warm. They can, at a pinch, be reheated the next day, but they are better the first.

Home-made cheese straws, made with the best French buttery puff pastry, stratospherically light and twisted with such a liberal scattering of Parmesan that it forms a golden-crusted lattice and the straws are conjoined like rows of Siamese twins, are just one of those more-ish can't-stop-eating kind of things that whet the appetite and satisfy concomitantly. There are some good all-butter puff pastries on the market now, so don't settle for anything less if you don't want to make your own. The rest is a few minutes work for infinite pleasure. Just how life should be once in a while.

These are a hit of something so more-ish, so flaky, so salt-sharp-hot they are everything you need with a glass of cold Fino or wine before the main event. You can make the dough really easily and roll it into a cylinder to chill in the fridge, cutting off discs of it every night when you want. You can also freeze the dough if you decide to make it well in advance and slice the biscuits as soon as the dough is defrosted enough for you to cut with a knife. A great non-starter of a starter – just make sure you make enough because no one will settle for just a couple.

PARMESAN, ANCHOVY AND CHILLI BISCUITS

MAKES ABOUT 24

3–4 red chillies, not the bird's-eye tongue blisterers
a smidgen of olive oil
110g/4oz plain organic flour

110g/4oz cold unsalted butter, cut into small cubes
50g/scant 2oz anchovies
110g/4oz Parmesan, freshly grated

Preheat the oven to 220°C/425°F/gas 7. Turn the chillies in a smidgen of olive oil before blistering the skins by holding them over a flame with a pair of tongs. If you don't have gas, you can hot roast the chillies until they are browned all over. Seal the chillies in a bag or put them in a small bowl covered with clingfilm. Leave until they're cool enough to peel, then seed and chop finely.

Sift the flour and either work the cubes of butter into it to crumb by hand or use a food processor. Chop the anchovies finely and mix them and the tiny flecks of chilli into the dough with the Parmesan. Knead to a paste, roll into a fat cylinder and wrap in foil to chill in the fridge as you would pastry.

Cut into slices about the thickness of a fat pound coin and place on Bakewell paper on a baking tray. Leave space between them as they will spread. Cook for about 10 minutes or until golden but not brown. Using a palette knife, move them straight onto a wire rack to firm up. Eat while they are still warm.

Roasting beetroots in foil keeps them looking like gloriously intense garnet-like jewels and preserves their sweet earthiness to perfection. Keep their whiskery bits on when you clean them, then no beetroot blood will bleed away as they cook. Everyone adds soured cream or crème fraîche to beetroot soups, but I like this pure and simple: a good strong stock, the beetroots and fronds of fresh dill.

ROASTED BEETROOT AND DILL SOUP

SERVES 4

6–8 medium beetroots

1 litre/1¾ pints good jellied chicken stock (see page 194)

sea salt and black pepper

fresh dill, finely chopped

Preheat the oven to 200°C/400°F/gas 6. Wash the beetroots, leaving on the whiskery bits, wrap them in foil and roast on a baking tray in the hot oven until they are soft when you pierce them right the way through with a skewer. Remove them from the foil, push off the skins with your fingers and chop the beetroot into cubes.

Throw the cubed beetroot into the liquidiser with the boiling hot stock, a little of each at a time, and whizz. Reheat and season, but don't prolong the cooking time or let the soup boil or it will change colour. Serve with a pinch of fresh green dill in the middle of each bowl.

I make this classic chowder with beautiful carpetshell clams from the Devon coast. All creamy salt-sweetness with a little added starchiness from the potatoes and smoky crispness from the rashers, this is a perfect starter or can make a more substantial lunch or supper dish if you up the quantity.

NEW ENGLAND CLAM CHOWDER

SERVES 4

2kg/4½lb clams
1 shallot, chopped
1 stick of celery, roughly chopped
2 rashers organic smoked streaky bacon
1 medium onion, finely chopped
a little sprig of thyme (enough for ½ tbsp)
1 bay leaf

30g/1oz unsalted butter
3 smallish potatoes, peeled and cut into
 1cm/½ in cubes
170ml/6fl oz double cream
sea salt and black pepper
1 tbsp chopped flat-leaf parsley

Put the clams into a large pan with a cup of cold water, the shallot and celery. Steam over a fierce heat until all the clams have opened. Pour the cooking liquor through a sieve and set it aside. Remove the clams from their shells once they have cooled down a little.

Snip the bacon rashers into small pieces with a pair of scissors and cook them in the pan until the fat runs. Stir in the finely chopped onion, thyme, bay leaf and butter and cook until the onions have turned translucent. Add the reserved clam liquor and the potatoes and simmer until the potatoes are cooked through.

Stir in the clams and cream and simmer for 4–5 minutes before seasoning and adding the parsley. Serve with bread or American-style, with crackers.

THE MAIN COURSE

2

RISOTTO BALSAMICO

SERVES 2

2 tbsp extra virgin olive oil
30g/1oz unsalted butter
1 small shallot, finely minced
1 stick of celery, strung and finely minced
225g/8oz Carnaroli rice
a small glass of dry white Italian wine

up to 850ml/1½ pints intense home-made
  chicken stock (see page 194)
more unsalted butter for finishing the risotto
freshly grated Parmesan
sea salt and black pepper
best balsamic vinegar

You need the most expensive, velvety, mellow balsamic vinegar for this – mine is a 20 year old. The thin, sharp stuff good enough for a salad dressing just won't do here. It has to be sweetly sticky, viscose and mellow.

Heat the olive oil and butter together in a shallow pan. I have a special Le Creuset cast-iron risotto pan with an enamelled inside; the large surface area helps the rice to cook evenly. When the oil and butter begin to bubble, add the finely minced shallot and celery and a little salt and stir them gently until they just begin to soften. Meanwhile heat the wine in a separate pan. Throw in the risotto rice and keep stirring to coat it with the oil and butter, then add the heated white wine. Stir as it bubbles and begins to be absorbed by the rice. Now add the hot chicken stock, a ladle or two at a time. The rice will take around 22 minutes to cook, but the one thing you cannot afford to do is to stop stirring for more than a minute at a time. The stirring is what releases the starch from the rice and gives it the lovely gloopy, starchy texture that a fine risotto should have.

When the risotto is still just al dente, or has bite to it, add a final ladle of stock with a knob of butter, a good handful of grated Parmesan and a scrunch of pepper, white if you are being a purist colour-wise. Put the lid on and remove the pan from the heat. Leave for 5 minutes for all the flavours to mingle and settle before giving the risotto a final stir.

Put a good tablespoon of best balsamic in the base of each shallow bowl, then carefully heap a mound of white risotto over it. The edges of the puddle should form a black moat around the white mound. Serve with extra cheese in a bowl if you like, though I don't think you need it. Each spoonful of rice and balsamic has the perfect contrast and needs no addition or embellishment. Perhaps serve a salad of pure white, shaved raw fennel afterwards, with an olive oil and lemon dressing, if this is going to be your main course.

This dish is the equivalent of serving caviar in a baked potato. It has just that kind of tongue-in-cheek, rich peasant quality to it, rather like wearing mink with cheap trainers. If it seemed showily self-conscious, I wouldn't put it on the plate, but the witty pretend-parsimony is part of its appeal. I have made more kinds of risotto than I could ever begin to count, with whatever ingredients or leftovers a forage through the fridge could provide. I had rather thought that after the more obvious white truffle, asparagus, lobster and crab, Vacherin, nero and seafood, clam, fennel, porcini, marrow bone and the like, risotto inspiration was more than

SIMPLE PASTA DISHES

At least once a week I look in my store cupboard and fridge and try to make something out of nothing for supper. Nine times out of ten that something is with pasta. More often than not, this is the most creative and frugal night of my culinary week; more often than not, I end up learning something new about what flavours and textures work with what kind of pasta. And more often than not, the children enjoy their supper more than on any other night of the week, even if it is meatless and unfishy.

What a cuisine the Italians have – unequalled in my experience, in terms of making something cheap, but nourishing and delicious, without going near a shop; something that has guts, heart and flavour and doesn't appear to have been cobbled together in a mix and matchless way. Oil, garlic, chilli pepper; butter and Parmesan; lemon, herbs and cream; sausage, garlic, tomatoes and cream; cabbage and potato; breadcrumbs, tomatoes and anchovies; Fontina, Gruyère and Parmesan; lemon zest, basil, goat's cheese and roasted tomatoes; roast squash, sage and chilli; pine nuts, basil, garlic and Parmesan… Here are peasant ingredients turned to gold once coupled with pasta, as long as you have good Parmesan, butter and olive oil in the first place.

From being a country that only knew spaghetti Bolognese, lasagne and macaroni cheese until 20 years ago, we now seem to eat as much pasta with as many different sauces and accompaniments as the Italians themselves. If only we had their climate, we could match their sott'olios and preserved tomatoes, artichokes and peppers, and have store cupboards brimming with glass jars full of the scent of summer to fall back on in the dead of winter.

SPAGHETTI WITH BREADCRUMBS AND ANCHOVIES

SERVES 4

255g/9oz ripe fresh tomatoes
2 cloves of garlic, finely sliced
1 tsp finely chopped dried chillies, seeds removed
1 tbsp chopped flat-leaf parsley
6 tbsp extra virgin olive oil
450g/1lb spaghetti or linguine

4 salted anchovies, de-spined and desalinated,
  or 8 bottled anchovy fillets, drained
30g/1oz unsalted butter
6 tbsp dried breadcrumbs
1 tsp dried oregano
zest of an organic lemon

Peel, halve, seed and chop the tomatoes. Put the garlic, chillies, parsley and half the olive oil in a large frying pan and sauté for a minute. Add the chopped tomatoes and cook over a medium heat for 5 minutes, stirring frequently. Meanwhile, cook the pasta according to the instructions on the packet.

Chop the anchovy fillets. Put all but a tablespoon of the rest of the olive oil into a small pan and heat, then add the anchovies and mash them down into the pan for a minute until they disintegrate into the oil. In a separate pan, melt the butter with the remaining oil and add the breadcrumbs, frying them until they turn golden and crisped. Throw the anchovies and their juice into the tomato mixture. Add the oregano and carry on cooking for a minute. Check the seasoning, then take the pan off the heat. Drain the pasta, but not too thoroughly, and put it back in the pot with a little of its cooking water still dripping from it. Add the tomato and anchovy mixture, give it a good stir and sprinkle the buttered breadcrumbs over the top before serving. A little zested lemon over the surface adds a lovely sherbetty zing at this stage.

In her great work, *Gastronomy of Italy*, Anna Del Conte explains that in the poor regions of southern Italy, toasted breadcrumbs were, and often still are, used instead of expensive Parmesan or Pecorino cheese. We also use bread sauce to eke out the meat, and we serve toasted, buttered breadcrumbs with a number of dishes both savoury and sweet: with our roast game birds, for example; with cauliflower and broccoli; or in an apple brown Betty. Anna uses dried breadcrumbs toasted, but I like to cook mine in a little mixed butter and olive oil so that they coat the pasta and have crunch. I also like to add a little lemon zest at the finish. This way with pasta is referred to by Anna as pasta con la mollica.

TAGLIATELLE WITH LEMON AND HERB SAUCE

SERVES 4

55g/2oz unsalted butter, plus an extra knob the size of a walnut
grated zest and juice of an organic lemon
up to 240ml/8fl oz double cream
sea salt and black pepper

1 heaped tbsp each of three of the following: finely chopped rosemary, sage, chives, tarragon, parsley or summer savory, or some torn basil
450g/1lb fresh or dried egg tagliatelle
110g/4oz Parmesan, finely grated

Melt the butter in a little pan and add the lemon zest, cream, seasoning and herbs. Bring slowly to the boil and simmer for a few minutes. Add the lemon juice and bring just to scald point. Remove the sauce from the heat and keep warm.

Cook the pasta in plenty of boiling salted water until al dente, then drain, but not completely. Put the pasta back in the pot with a little of its cooking water still dripping from it and throw in the extra knob of butter. Pour the sauce over the pasta, add a handful of the Parmesan and toss well. Serve with a bowl of the remaining Parmesan to pass around.

SPAGHETTI AL CACIO E PEPE

SERVES 4

450g/1lb spaghetti
3 tbsp extra virgin olive oil, a good one like Ravida, Seggiano or Nuñez de Prado

coarsely ground black pepper
85g/3oz Pecorino Romano, grated

Bring a large pan of salted water to the boil and throw in the pasta. Cook it for only 5 minutes before draining, but save the cooking water in another pan. Pour the olive oil into the hot pan, add the pasta and return to the heat, adding a ladleful of the hot cooking water from time to time and the coarsely ground black pepper. Once the pasta is cooked al dente, add the grated Pecorino and stir it in thoroughly. Check the seasoning and serve.

Another plain Jane but perfect dish – the crucial ingredient is Pecorino Romano, the lovely salt, crystalline, aged sheep's milk cheese that has a lactic graininess and strength of flavour enough to make this dish, with no need for further partnering. Just black pepper and good olive oil.

SEA BASS BAKED WITH LEMONGRASS AND DILL

SERVES 4

1 x 1.5kg/3¼lb or thereabouts fresh wild sea bass
a sprig of fresh dill
a couple of lemongrass stalks
1 tbsp chopped flat-leaf parsley
55g/2oz softened butter

zest of a lemon and a spritz of its juice
4 tbsp breadcrumbs
olive oil
a splosh of white wine
sea salt and black pepper

Ask your fishmonger to scale and gut the fish, having made sure it is bright and beady eyed, as it were, the flesh gluey and shiny, not dull, drab and dry looking. Preheat the oven to 180°C/350°F/gas 4. Wash the fish inside and out under a cold tap. Lay a sheet of foil large enough to make a baggy parcel for the fish on a roasting tray.

Strip the dill from its stalks and chop finely – you need about a tablespoon. Unfurl the lemongrass until you have only the inner, bendy, juicy core of it and chop it finely; the exterior is too tough to eat. Mash the dill, lemongrass and parsley into the softened butter with the zest of the lemon and a spritz of juice, salt and pepper. Mash in the breadcrumbs and a little olive oil if the butter is difficult to work with the breadcrumbs.

Score deep, diagonal slashes at intervals along one side of the fish – about four, depending on its length – and stuff the herbed butter in with your fingers as best you can. Turn the fish over and do the same on its other side. If there is any butter left, stuff it into the cavity where the fish has been gutted. Add a good splosh of white wine and a little libation of oil to the fish, then season the skin.

Close and seal the parcel – it should be baggy but tightly sealed. Bake the fish in the oven for about 35 minutes, or until a knife point or skewer penetrates the whole fish at its widest girth; it should be consistently soft right the way through. Open the parcel and leave for 15 minutes, then serve the fish in fillets with some of the juice poured over them.

A whole, silvery-scaled wild sea bass, as bright as metallic foil, is a beautiful fish to behold and to eat, and one best left as plain as possible so that its tender, subtle flesh tastes of itself. I always cook fish on the bone if I possibly can, therein lies the best flavour. In the case of the bass, it is best left for 10–15 minutes after you have removed it from the oven for the flesh to firm up. Serving fish warm, or even at room temperature, is something you don't need to be afraid of.

WARM GRIDDLED CHICKEN WITH GREEN OLIVE SALSA

SERVES 4

4 large, organic chicken legs or 4 thighs
2 tbsp olive oil
juice of half a lemon
sea salt and black pepper

For the salsa
90ml/3fl oz best extra virgin olive oil
225g/8oz green olives, pitted and chopped finely

2 stalks of celery, strung with a potato peeler and
  finely diced
1 tbsp red wine vinegar
2 cloves of garlic, finely minced
1 red chilli, quartered, seeded and finely diced
grated zest of an organic lemon
2 tbsp coarsely chopped flat-leaf parsley
black pepper

Start with the salsa. Put all the ingredients in a bowl and turn them with your hands before leaving them for at least 30 minutes. Stir everything together once more just before you serve the salsa on top of the meat.

Turn the chicken pieces thoroughly in the olive oil and lemon juice and rub the seasoning well into the skin with your fingers. Whack them on a heated griddle, turning them after 10 minutes and cooking until a skewer pierces them with no resistance and no bloodiness, or cook them in the usual way on your barbecue. If you have neither option, cook them under a grill, but the results will not be quite the same, obviously.

This is a lovely light summer supper or lunch dish, which is best eaten at room temperature, so the charred juices from the chicken mingle with the piquancy of olives, undramatic heat from the chilli and the oily, lemony, parsleyed undercurrents. Make the salsa before you cook the chicken; it needs to develop its flavour for at least 30 minutes after it has been made. The salsa is also good over a chunk of plain roasted white fish like cod, or some wings of skate poached in acidulated water. Only the plumpest, oiliest, most meaty green olives will do for this dish; I use Seggiano's Bella di Cerignola olives (for stockists, phone 020 7272 5588 or see their website: www.seggiano.co.uk). You can also serve this salsa with tiny raw or briefly blanched and peeled broad beans in the early summer, in which case a couple of finely minced anchovies added to the salsa is a delectable variation. Use chicken legs or thighs, not the ubiquitous skinless, tasteless chicken breasts, please. All meat cooked on the bone tastes better, and without fat and skin the chicken will dry out horribly.

VIVIENNE WALTERS' JAMAICAN JERK CHICKEN

SERVES 4

1 onion, chopped into small chunks
3 spring onions
1 Scotch bonnet or hot pepper
4 cloves of garlic
3 sprigs of thyme

1 tsp pimento seeds
1 tsp sea salt
1 tsp black pepper
60ml/2fl oz dark soy sauce
1 x 1.8 kg/4lb organic chicken, jointed

Put all the ingredients except the chicken in a food processor and blend together. Pour the marinade over the chicken joints, cover with clingfilm and leave in the fridge overnight.

The next day, bring the chicken back to room temperature and preheat the oven to its hottest setting. Put the chicken joints in their sauce in a roasting tin and cook for 20 minutes before reducing the temperature to 180°C/350°F/gas 4 for an hour. Simple. Vivienne serves her chicken with basmati rice into which she throws some peas and some steamed broccoli or carrots.

Just the name, Jamaican Jerk Chicken, is evocative. This is the real deal, from Vivienne who comes from Stony Hill, St Andrew in Jamaica and is living in Manhattan, working her way back home. Vivienne prepares her jerk on a Saturday night, marinating it ready for a party on Sunday. You may cook it in the oven or on the barbecue grill.

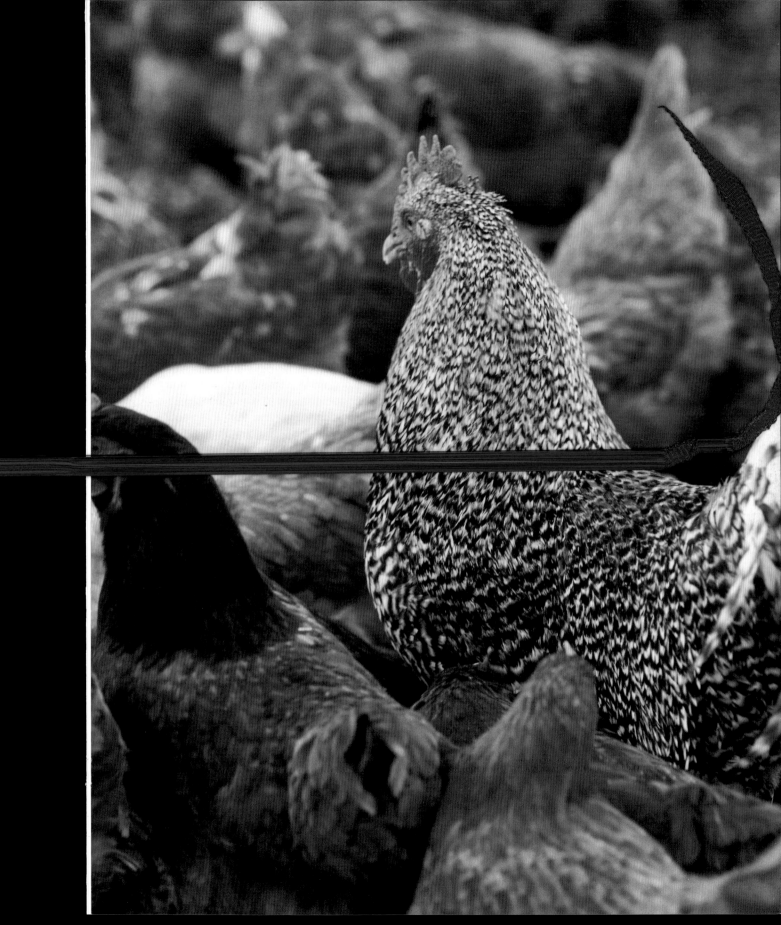

PHEASANT IN A POT WITH SOMERSET CIDER BRANDY

SERVES 4–6

6 rashers smoked streaky bacon, snipped into
  small strips
olive oil
85g/3oz unsalted butter
a brace of pheasants, usually a cock and a hen
1 large onion, chopped small
12 bruised juniper berries
1 tbsp thyme leaves
2 cloves of garlic

225g/8oz organic whole barley
sea salt and black pepper
bottle Kingston Black single-estate cider, or a dry,
  non-commercial cider
6 Coxes or similar sharp eating apples
lemon juice
1 tbsp molasses sugar
2 tbsp Somerset Cider Brandy, Calvados or Cognac
1 heaped tbsp crème fraîche

Preheat the oven to 180°C/350°F/gas 4. Fry the snipped rashers alone in a heavy-bottomed pan that will fit the two birds and all else besides in with them. Cook over a medium heat until the fat begins to run and the strips begin to crisp and brown. Push the bacon to the side and lob in a tablespoon or so of olive oil and about 30g/1oz butter. Let these foam and fizz before browning the pheasants on all sides. Remove the birds to a plate.

Add the onion to the pan, coating it in the oil and butter, then the bruised juniper berries and thyme leaves. Add the chopped garlic and the barley, season and stir to coat it all over. Pour in two-thirds of the heated cider and bring it all just to the boil.

Plunge the birds breast down into the melee and cover with a circle of greaseproof paper, cut to fit inside the pan, and a lid. Put in the oven for 20 minutes. Then remove the covers, check the barley, which will have swollen and absorbed a lot of the liquid, turn it and add more hot cider and a little chicken stock if the level isn't at least half way up the barley and pheasants. Return to the oven for 20–30 minutes. Test the birds by pulling gently on a leg from each bird, which should ease away from the carcass, and see how raw the inner side of the legs looks. They should be pink, but not bloodily so, and not resistant to a skewer. When cooked, remove the birds to rest on a carving board under foil. Taste the barley – it may still be too al dente, in which case return it to the oven for 10 minutes or until cooked.

Meanwhile, start the apples. Peel, quarter and core them, and slice thickly. Squeeze over a little lemon juice to stop them discolouring. In a heavy-bottomed frying pan, melt about 55g/2oz unsalted butter and add the apple slices when it begins to foam. Sprinkle over a tablespoon of molasses sugar and turn up the heat so that it begins to caramelise. At this point, splosh over the brandy and with due ceremony, light a taper, stand back and set light to it to burn off the alcohol. Once the flames have died down, check the apples, which should still be quite crisp, slosh over the crème fraîche and stir it into the juices. Remove the pan from the heat and cover.

Carve the birds by simply jointing each leg at its meeting point with the carcass and taking off each breast whole. Place the grain mountain in the middle of a heated serving platter and put the jointed birds on top with a little more thyme for green speckle if you like. Surround with a necklace of creamy apples and serve. A perfect winter potful.

I had a brace of pheasants from my friends the Woods on Exmoor, which I knew would have been hung just how I like them – that is, to gameyness, not greenness. I could have roasted them, but I prefer the less exacting nature of

SWEET-SOUR ROASTED PARSNIPS AND SWEET POTATOES

SERVES 4

2 large parsnips
2 large sweet potatoes
2 tbsp olive oil
2 tsp sesame oil

1 dsrtsp pomegranate molasses
1 tbsp runny thyme or other intense, dark honey
sea salt and black pepper

Preheat the oven to 200°C/400°F/gas 6. Peel and cut the vegetables into chunky batons – you do not need to par-boil the parsnips for this recipe. Put them on a shallow baking tray and pour over both oils, turning the batons over to coat all sides completely. Dribble over a thin stream of pomegranate molasses, followed by a thin stream of honey and turn to coat evenly. Season and put straight into the oven.

After 20 minutes, when the vegetables will have stickily blackened patches (and so will the baking tray), scrape the residue over the vegetables and turn them over. Roast for another 20 minutes or until both sides of the vegetable batons are equally crusted and cooked through to a caramelised, burnished finish.

I had hoped to roast this lovely winter combination of salmon-pink sweet potato and creamy parsnip with sesame seeds and honey, but the seeds I had were past their sell-by date! Then I thought again. Honey always brings out the sweetness of the already sweet rooty vegetables, particularly if it is a dark, intensely flavoured one. What if I added a little pomegranate molasses to sharpen and deepen the flavour and some sesame oil to compensate? The result – sticky, sharp, sweet, gooey, blackened roots with that great combination of soft yielding and firm crunch.

PARTRIDGE IN CABBAGE

SERVES 4

4 small heads of early cabbage, halved horizontally
55g/2oz unsalted butter
a little olive oil
4 partridges

3–4 crushed juniper berries
sea salt and black pepper
1 glass of port

Preheat the oven to 180°C/350°F/gas 4. Scoop out the insides of each halved cabbage with your fingers and a small knife, making just enough space for the birds to fit in between the two halves. Remove as much of the core as you can without the cabbage falling apart, that way the cabbage will cook through. Melt the butter in a heavy-bottomed pot that will hold all four heads of cabbage stuffed with partridge in a single layer, and brown the partridges on all sides briefly, seasoning them as you go.

Now put each bird inside a cabbage half and return the halves to the pot with the juniper berries. Briefly sauté them in the butter and oil to begin wilting the cabbage leaves. Put on the cabbage lids, turn the cabbage and partridge over to brown the other cabbage half a little and add the port, allowing it to bubble a little. Throw the torn or chopped remains of the scooped-out cabbage around the four cabbage heads. Cover the pot with a lid and cook in the oven for 30 minutes. The birds should be pinkly tender when pierced with a skewer.

The cabbage will have shrunk down and should be all juicy and buttery. Serve everyone with one whole cabbage and partridge and a heap of creamy, mashed potatoes.

An English partridge, early in the season when it is still young, is one of the joys of autumn. Although they are wonderful roasted, I wanted to find a way to keep the birds tender and juicy and to pair them with something that brought out their shy, gamey flavour without drowning it. Early heads of cabbage and a little port seemed a good idea. Then I thought, why not scoop out the centre of the cabbages and shelter the little birds, already browned, inside them? I covered them with the other scooped-out cabbage halves to seal them in and prevent them drying out. It worked first time, and my younger daughter Charissa and I sat down to a feast.

DUCK BRAISED WITH GRAPES

SERVES 4

1 x 2.2kg/5lb free-range duck
3 rashers organic green streaky bacon, snipped
  into strips
1 large onion, chopped
1 large carrot, chopped
1 stalk celery, strung and chopped
1 tbsp good runny honey

1kg/2¼lb organic seedless grapes
juice of a lemon
2 strips organic orange peel, no pith
1 star anise
sea salt and black pepper
150ml/5fl oz stock made with the duck giblets

Preheat the oven to 220°C/425°F/gas 7. Prick the duck all over with a fork, then place it in a roasting tin, breast up, and roast it for 45 minutes. Once the duck fat has started to run into the roasting tin, pour a few tablespoons of fat into a large, heavy-bottomed pot that the duck will fit into and fry the bacon for a few minutes, followed by the chopped vegetables. When they have begun to brown, pour in the honey and turn to coat the vegetables as they begin to caramelise.

Put the duck on top of the vegetables and add the grapes around it, pushing them down. Squeeze in the lemon juice, add the orange peel, star anise, salt and pepper and pour over the hot stock. Bring to the boil, cover with a circle of greaseproof, cut to fit inside the pot, and the lid, and put it into the oven for an hour. This will give you a cooked, not rare, duck, but you can shorten the cooking and lengthen the resting time if you wish, leaving the vegetables and grapes in the oven while you do so.

Put the grapes, vegetables and bacon with all the stock, excluding the peel and star anise, through the coarse blade of a mouli, then heat it through and check the seasoning. Carve the duck – the legs into two pieces each, the breasts likewise. Serve with a great bowl of buttery mashed potato. An orange and chicory salad to finish with works well too.

Elizabeth David had a wonderful recipe gleaned from the French winegrowers called 'queue de boeuf des vignerons' – winegrowers' oxtail, or, more simply translated, oxtail stewed with grapes. The slow cooking to release the almost oily, gelatinous fatness of the oxtail, spliced with the sweet acidity of the grape, makes a fantastically rich, sticky winter dish. I think duck, which works well with so many different fruits, is as good a meat as oxtail to combine with sweet vegetables, in this case carrots, onions and grapes. Rather than browning the duck in pieces as you would the oxtail, it is better to par-roast it so that all the fat starts to run and can be used for browning the vegetables, then to braise it to succulent sweet-sharp tenderness with the coarsely moulied grape sauce.

Figs and fat meat – there is something about the combination, whether it be the lardo- or prosciutto-wrapped piggy figgies on page 84, or figs soaked with the rich succulence of duck fat and cut with dry, palate-sharpening port. It simply works. Remember to start this dish 24 hours in advance, as the figs need to be well and truly pickled in port.

DUCK BRAISED IN PORT WITH BLACK FIGS

SERVES 6

24 black figs
port
1 x 2.2kg/5lb duck and its giblets
6 sprigs of thyme

300ml/10fl oz veal stock, or game or chicken stock will do (see pages 194 and 196)
sea salt and black pepper

The day before you want to cook this dish, stand the figs upright, packed cheek by jowl, in a dish, and pour port over them to halfway up their sides. Cover with clingfilm and turn every few hours or whenever you remember.

Twenty-four hours later, preheat the oven to 190°C/375°F/gas 5. Prick the duck all over with a skewer and brown it on all sides in a roasting pan on top of the stove. Strip the thyme from its stems and add to the pan so that the leaves begin to release their oils in the duck fat. Now place the duck, breast up, on a trivet in the roasting pan and season it with salt and pepper. Roast in the hot oven for 20 minutes, then turn the duck over and pour over half the port. After another 20 minutes turn the duck breast side up again and add the rest of the port. Cook for 20 minutes more, then add half the stock and 15 minutes later, the rest of the stock. Then plop in the figs for the last 15 minutes. These timings are not critical, only a rough guide. You do not want the duck to dry out at any stage and you don't want the figs to collapse to a pulp.

An hour and a half to an hour and three-quarters of cooking time should render the duck perfectly braised and the figs cooked in the hot, sticky, thyme-laced liquor. Carve the duck and set it on a warmed serving plate surrounded by a black guard of figs.

Meanwhile, reduce the juices further and serve them separately in a dégraisseur so that you are not put off by the duck fat. You may like to sop up the juices with a celeriac and potato purée or with potato alone, or you may prefer to serve just a salad with some chicory, peppery watercress and sliced oranges.

SALTIMBOCCA ALLA ROMANA

SERVES AS MANY AS YOU WISH

1 escalope of free-range or organic veal per
  person, battered and flattened by your butcher
a slice of best Parma ham for each escalope,
  San Daniele or similar
2 sage leaves per person

seasoned flour
unsalted butter
sea salt and black pepper
white wine

Spread the escalopes out flat on a board and cover each slice completely with a slice of Parma ham, including its fatty edge. Place two sage leaves next to each other in the middle of each slice and weave a cocktail stick in and out of each of the three layers to hold them together. Put each escalope into a ziploc bag with some seasoned flour just before you are ready to cook, then take them out and shake off the excess.

Melt some butter in a frying pan large enough to hold several escalopes in one go, or use two pans if you need to. Put in the escalopes and brown on one side for a couple of minutes. Turn them over and repeat, making sure you remove the escalopes to a hot serving dish the moment they are tender right through when pierced with a skewer. Add a sprinkle of salt and a grind of black pepper.

Now de-glaze the pan with a good glug of white wine, scraping the pan juices and butter as you go and reducing the wine until you have a scant, gluey tablespoon of liquor for each escalope. I serve mine with a potato and celeriac purée, a gratin of fennel and a stunning Piemontese side dish of baked figs and lardo (see page 84).

Make the potato and celeriac mash with two-thirds potato to one-third celeriac, a very little butter, and some of the water you have cooked the vegetables in to moisten the purée. A little nutmeg and salt and pepper are all you need, no milk or cream.

There is the old-fashioned retro way and the more modern way to serve this delicious gluey, salty, sagey dish. Its three layers of flavour are a perfect triumvirate: the medicinal astringence of sage, the porky, cured saltiness of the Parma ham and the tender, palely subtle tones of the veal, floured, seasoned and buttery, with a scant de-glazing of white wine. I made both when researching the dish for this book: the old-style roll-up and tether with a cocktail stick version, and the flat-on-its-back-and-spear-the-sage version. The latter was far and away the more successful. The roll-up doesn't cook the sage; the flat frazzles it delectably. The roll-up doesn't crisp up the prosciutto; the flat version does.

GRATIN OF FENNEL

1 large head of fennel per person
unsalted butter and olive oil

sea salt and black pepper
1 tbsp freshly grated Parmesan per fennel bulb

Preheat the oven to 190°C/375°F/gas 5. Remove the tough outer leaves of the fennel ruthlessly, then slice the bulbs down through their core so the leaves don't part company with the base. Depending on the size of the bulbs you may wish to quarter them.

Steam the fennel pieces until just resistant when pierced through with a skewer and place them cut side down in a gratin dish. Sprinkle with olive oil and a few little pieces of butter, season and throw over the grated Parmesan. Bake for 15–20 minutes or until golden and bubbling.

PIGGY FIGGIES OR FIGS IN LARDO

1 or 2 black figs per person

lardo or prosciutto fat

Preheat the oven to 220°C/425°F/gas 7. Simply open the tops of the figs out gently and wind a little lardo or fat through and over the top of them, a strip or two per fig. Place on a baking tray and blast for 3 minutes, by which time the fat will have both crisped and leaked its porky, salt juices into the grainy, red cavity of the black fig.

Sexy, moreish, the most perfect soft and crisp, salt and sweet bite you ever came across. A great taste to serve with drinks or as a starter as well as a side-dish.

Lardo is difficult to come by outside Italy or a good Italian deli, but the fat from some sliced prosciutto works well wound in thin skeins around the figs. This is a dish Rob and I first chanced upon at a lovely Michelin-starred restaurant in the hills of Santo Stefano Belbo in Piemonte. The figs were served with braised veal cheek, which fell from the fork it was so stewily soft. We liked the dish so much we ordered second helpings.

STUFFED BREAST OF VEAL

SERVES 6

1 breast of veal with its bones; boned weight of the meat should be about 1kg/2¼lb

2 thick slices of good white bread, crusts removed

1 egg, beaten

1 large bulb fennel with its fronds, chopped into dice

olive oil

1 heaped tsp fennel seeds

110g/4oz pork mince

12 large green olives, pitted and roughly chopped

nutmeg

grated zest of an organic lemon

sea salt and black pepper

2 cloves of garlic, finely chopped

2 onions, finely chopped

veal stock, or chicken stock will do (see pages 194 and 196)

white wine

Lay the veal out flat on your chopping board. Dip the bread, torn into large chunks, into the beaten egg on a plate and put it on top of the veal, squashing it into the veal to flatten it slightly. Gently sauté the fennel in a little olive oil in a pan until it begins to soften and turn translucent, then scatter in the fennel seeds and cook for another minute. Place the warm fennel on top of the bread. Mix the pork and green olives (I like the Seggiano ones) and press them into another thin layer on top of the fennel, then zest the lemon over them, season and add the finely chopped garlic. Do not allow any of the ingredients to go too close to the edge of the veal, or they will tumble out when you roll it up into a parcel.

Roll up the veal and tie it with string all the way along. It is perfectly possible to do this on your own. I do a sort of bastardised blanket stitch and push all the ingredients into the centre as they try to escape! Any real escapees can be tossed into the pot.

While you are doing this, have the veal bones and any extra large marrowbones browning in a roasting tin in a hot oven. This takes 20–30 minutes, during which time they will also leak a delicious amount of fat. Turn the oven down to 140°C/275°F/gas 1. Pour the fat into the large, heavy-bottomed pot you are going to cook the veal in and brown the roll of veal swiftly on all sides. Now brown the chopped onion until it is just beginning to soften and tuck the bones around the breast. Heat the veal stock and white wine, equal amounts of both, and add enough to come halfway up the meat and bones. Cover with a circle of greaseproof paper that just fits inside the pan and a lid, and braise for 2½–3 hours.

Remove the meat from the pot and place it on a carving board. Keep the oniony juices hot on top of the stove. Carve into lovely slices marbled with the stuffing, ladle juices over each plateful and serve with a dark green and an orange vegetable for colour relief and some buttery mash.

Every time I go to Italy or France I eat veal, as though it were as rare a treasure as a truffle. Also, because veal is so much more a part of the daily life of a restaurant or a home there, the cooking of it is so confident, be it anything from a slow- or quick-cooked cut, a sweetbread, an escalope, a kidney or the greatest dish of all, ossobuco, the bone with the hole in the middle. There are very few places here to buy good veal that has been reared

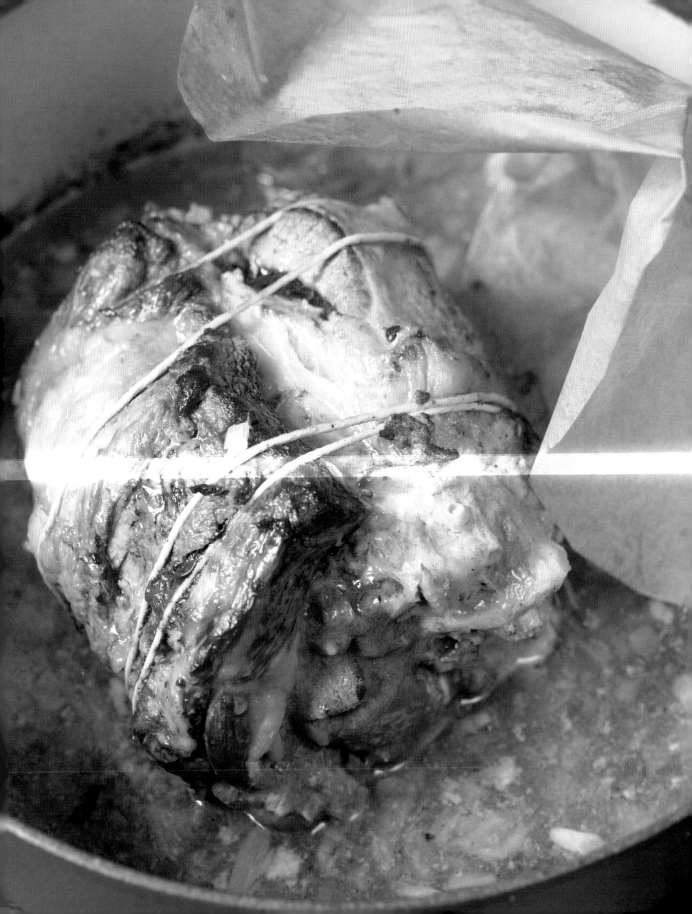

properly, tenderly, kindly, to tenderness, as it were, but Heal Farm at King's Nympton in Devon, run by Anne and Richard Petch, was the first and is still a yardstick (phone 01769 574341 or see www.healfarm.co.uk for details). Veal doesn't have to be expensive. This recipe for breast of veal, boned out but with the bones kept for browning and flavouring the dish with its gorgeously gluey, marrowy goodness, uses one of the cheaper cuts. I have always found the affinity between veal and fennel irresistible. Here it is exaggerated with the intensely musky, medicinal fennel seeds, not just the Florentine bulbs and their feathery fronds.

VEAL RAGU

SERVES 2

2 cooked ossibuchi and whatever leftover jellied stock with onions you have, or use chopped cold roast veal or 225g/8oz veal mince
1 onion, finely chopped
1 tbsp olive oil
4 cloves of garlic, finely chopped
1 x 400g/13oz tin tomatoes
a glass of red wine or Marsala

2 bay leaves
110–170g/4–6oz Parmesan, freshly grated
sea salt and fresh black pepper
450g/1lb good penne, the best is extruded through bronze dies so that the pasta sauce will cling to the ridges and rills in it; the longer the cooking time on the instructions, the better the quality of the pasta

First, wiggle and push and prod the marrow out of the bones, then chop it very finely with the cooked meat from the shanks. I do not have a mincer, and I think that very finely chopped meat is best for this dish – it gives a bite you don't get from mince.

Sauté the finely chopped onion in a tablespoon of olive oil until it begins to soften, then add the finely chopped cloves of garlic and a little salt. When they have both begun to soften, tip in the meat and stir and turn it before adding the tomatoes. Chop them down into the onion, then add a ladleful of jellied stock and the bay leaves. Simmer them together while the stock begins to reduce. After about 10 minutes, add the red wine, and continue to simmer down and stir from time to time. Cook the ragu for about 30 minutes, adding more stock if you need to, or more wine if you don't have enough stock. If you are using mince rather than ossibuchi, cook for an extra 30 minutes. I like this dish to have a good quota of liquid to meat, as the gluey juices will eventually adhere to the pasta and lubricate the finished dish. You can use Marsala if you prefer, which will sweeten the acidity of the tomatoes and carry through the Italian theme.

Cook the pasta in boiling salted water while the ragu is simmering away. When it is still just al dente, drain it, but not too thoroughly, and put it back into the pot with a little of its cooking liquor. Add the sauce and, over a very low heat, turn it into the penne, making sure that it is distributed right through and the tomatoey, winey juices are clinging to pasta. Throw a good handful of Parmesan into the finished dish in the pot and stir it in. Serve in warmed bowls with a bowl of Parmesan alongside for people to spoon over as they like.

This is a perfect way of using up leftover ossibuchi and the jellied, winey stock that will have intensified in flavour overnight. If you don't have ossibuchi or leftover roast veal, use veal mince.

This farm belongs to my neighbours, Sue and Andrew, and is home to dozens of deliciously chubby little Old Spot and Middle White porkers.

WILD BOAR (OR PORK) AND MOREL STEW

SERVES 4

1kg/2¼lb or thereabouts of wild boar fillet cut into large chunks, double the size of what you would use for stew ordinarily

3–4 tbsp seasoned flour in a ziploc bag

1 tbsp fresh rosemary or winter savory needles, chopped almost to powder

2 tbsp olive oil

a nut of butter

12 cipollini onions or shallots

2 tbsp balsamic vinegar

16 dried morels, rehydrated according to the instructions on the packet

red wine, heated

2 heaped tbsp crème fraîche

Throw the meat into the bag of seasoned flour and herbs and then remove it, piece by piece, shaking off any excess flour. Heat a heavy-bottomed, lidded pot and add the olive oil when the base is hot. When the oil is beginning to shudder, add the butter and then brown pieces of floured meat in a single layer in batches. Brown the meat on all sides at a medium heat. (Use all olive oil if you would rather.) Remove the meat to a plate.

Add the cipollini or shallots to the pan with a little more oil if you need it. Keep turning the onions to coat them and cook for about 4 minutes. Add a tablespoon of good balsamic vinegar and let it bubble and reduce before adding a second tablespoon. Add the soaked morels, without their soaking liquor, and the meat and enough hot wine just to cover; bring gradually to simmering point. Cover with a circle of greaseproof cut to fit inside the pot, just above the simmering stew, and a lid and cook at a mere blip for 40 minutes.

Add the crème fraîche to the pot and whisk it in as best you can to amalgamate with the winey juices. Cover the pot again and cook for a further 20–30 minutes or until the meat is spoon-tender when pierced with a skewer. Serve with lashings of mash and some green vegetables.

My favourite butcher in New York is Ottomanelli's on Bleecker Street. Their meat is properly reared, hung and butchered and on every trip to the shop both knives and wit are sharpened on a whetstone, New York style. Behind the Ottomanelli counter are Berkshire pigs, wild boar, venison, beef as black and ribboned with creamy fat as you could wish, mallard, sweetbreads (rare jewels here in England these days), ossibuchi, veal to roast, escalopes of veal and many other scarcity value things I love. This early autumn dish would work as well with pork. I would probably use cubed shoulder, even with a good, fatty, rare breed porker, so that the meat didn't dry out or lose its tenderness from lack of fat, as well as for the flavour.

BEEF AND BAROLO STEW

SERVES 8

2kg/4½lb best braising steak, cut into large cubes
seasoned flour
2 large onions, chopped
olive oil
4 sticks of celery, strung and sliced
4 large carrots, cut into 2cm/¾in lengths
6 cloves of garlic, peeled and left whole
2 large leeks, whites cut into thick discs

1 swede, peeled and cut into cubes
1 bottle Barolo or other robust red wine
2 x 400g/13oz tins whole organic tomatoes
sea salt and black pepper
a bouquet made with a large sprig of parsley,
   rosemary, thyme and 2 bay leaves with 2 strips
   orange peel, tied together

Preheat the oven to 150°C/300°F/gas 2. Throw the meat into a ziploc bag of well-seasoned flour and toss until it is well coated. Shake off any excess. Brown the meat in olive oil in batches, frying it in a single layer in a heavy-bottomed pan. Remove each batch to a plate as you go, adding more oil if you need to.

Now start frying the onions in more olive oil, adding a little salt at the outset so that they begin to release their juices. Add all the vegetables one by one in the given order, sautéing them gently until the onions have begun to soften and turn translucent. Return the meat to the pan and add the wine in two or three bursts, waiting for it to reach simmer point before you add the next slug. When the wine has just begun to simmer, pour in the tomatoes, chopping them down into the stew with a knife. The meat and vegetables should be pretty well covered by now. Season with salt and pepper and, when the stew comes back to a simmer, tuck in the bouquet. Cut out a sheet of greaseproof to fit on top of the stew in the pan and cover with a lid. Either simmer very gently for 3 hours on top of the stove or put it into the oven and do the same.

Prepare parsley and horseradish dumplings (see page 108) in time to cook them on top of the stew for the last 20 minutes of cooking time.

Beef in Barolo is one of the great Italian classics, paired here with that oft-spurned winter heft of dough, the dumpling. Flecked with green, tweedy parsley and a hidden hit of hot horseradish, gently fluffed up into a steaming cloud above the winey, stewy juices, the dumpling should not be neglected or seen as mere ballast or padding. A slightly gooey, sticky, crusty edge to the little dumplings' softness is the perfect texture alongside the spoon-soft shards of meat and the tender vegetables. All you need is a great hillock of buttery mash alongside. If Barolo is beyond your pocket, opt for a full-bodied, robust red wine.

This stew is always better the second day, so cool it and leave overnight if you can. I use wonderful Longhorn beef from Richard Vaughan (phone: 01600 890296 or see the website: www.huntsham.com for details).

This dish is not about flounces and flourishes of green or pink peppercorns or pools of double cream. It is about good rump steak, well aged and well hung, with a thick ribbon of fat; it is about crushed black peppercorns; and about Cognac and butter forming an alliance and turning into a glossy emulsion. Simple and classic. My steak comes from Richard Vaughan's Longhorn herd (see page 106 for details) and is well aged, exceptionally long-hung and full of flavour.

STEAK AU POIVRE

SERVES 2

2 tbsp black peppercorns or 1 tbsp each black and white peppercorns

2 good thick rump steaks, size according to your appetite

sea salt

1–2 tbsp olive oil

45g/1½oz unsalted butter

2 tbsp Cognac

Coarsely grind the peppercorns in a mortar, then put them in a sieve and sieve out the dusty powder – you don't want this on your meat as it would make it far too hot. Press the steaks down into the peppercorns on both sides as firmly as you can, although some will fall off, however hard you press. Sprinkle a little salt over both pieces of meat.

Heat 1–2 tablespoons of olive oil in a heavy-bottomed frying pan until it begins to smoke. Put the steaks in carefully and cook them for a couple of minutes. Turn the heat down to medium and continue to cook for another minute, then turn each steak over and cook it for another 3 minutes.

Remove the steaks to a warm plate and leave them somewhere warm to relax. Meanwhile, put 30g/1oz of the butter in the pan and wait for it to foam. Add a couple of tablespoons of good Cognac and whisk together, then add the rest of the butter in small pieces and whisk it in until the sauce looks glossy. Pour it over the steaks and serve with Lyonnaise potatoes and gratin of spinach (see page 114).

BUTTERNUT SQUASH AND CROTTIN DE CHAVIGNOL TART

SERVES 8 OR 6 GREEDY GUZZLERS

1 x 23cm/9in shortcrust pastry case, made with
  170g/6oz flour to 85g/3oz butter (see page 197)
1 small butternut squash, or red onion squash
3–4 tbsp double cream
2 eggs and 2 egg yolks

1 crottin de Chavignol or similar small aged
  goat's cheese
a small bunch of sage leaves
2–3 tbsp best olive oil
2 heaped tbsp crème fraîche
sea salt and black pepper

To make the pastry, sift the flour into a bowl or food processor and add the cold, cubed butter. Work quickly and lightly by hand, or pulse briefly to a crumb, before adding about 1 tablespoon of ice-cold water and working or pulsing quickly just to the point at which it coheres. Wrap the pastry in clingfilm and refrigerate for 30 minutes to an hour. For more on pastry, see page 197.

Seed the squash and roast it in a hot oven in wedges. When the flesh is soft, scoop it out and purée it in a food processor with the double cream. Beat in the eggs and egg yolks.

Preheat the oven to 200°C/400°F/gas 6. Bake the pastry blind for 15 minutes, then remove the foil and beans, dock the base and sides with the tines of a fork to stop them bubbling up, and return the pastry case the oven to dry out for 5 minutes.

Remove the thin, crusted rind of the crottin, halve it and break it into small, lumpy shards. Sprinkle these over the base of the tart . Heat the olive oil in a small pan and when it is fiercely hot, throw in the whole sage leaves, turning them quickly with a spoon so that they frazzle and crisp in a minute or two. Drain off the oil and place most of the leaves in the base of the tart case with the crottin. Set the rest aside. Beat the crème fraîche into the squash, cream and egg mixture and season well with black pepper and only a little salt – the crottin is salty.

Scrape the mixture into the tart case to just under the top of the pastry and strew the remaining frazzled sage on top. Turn the oven down to 180°C/375°F/gas 4 and bake until the tart is puffed up and magnificently burnished in patches. This will take 20–30 minutes – it should be set, but with a faint shudder. Place on a rack and cool for 20 minutes before eating while it is between hot and warm. That way you will really taste it. Serve with a salad of watercress or Treviso chicory – something a little bitter and peppery.

Since writing *The Art of the Tart* I have not rested on my reputation as the Queen of Tarts, though in some quarters this may not be considered a sobriquet worth selling one's soul for. *Tarts with Tops On* followed, a book of pies as sweet and savoury as its original companion. I still get carried away by the form, a veritable Bach of the food world, reliant as it is on structure, containment, restraint and secret beauty, all of which have to be harmonious and many faceted, as well as emotive of what really lies beneath. So, there I was during Thanksgiving week, cooking in the kitchen of

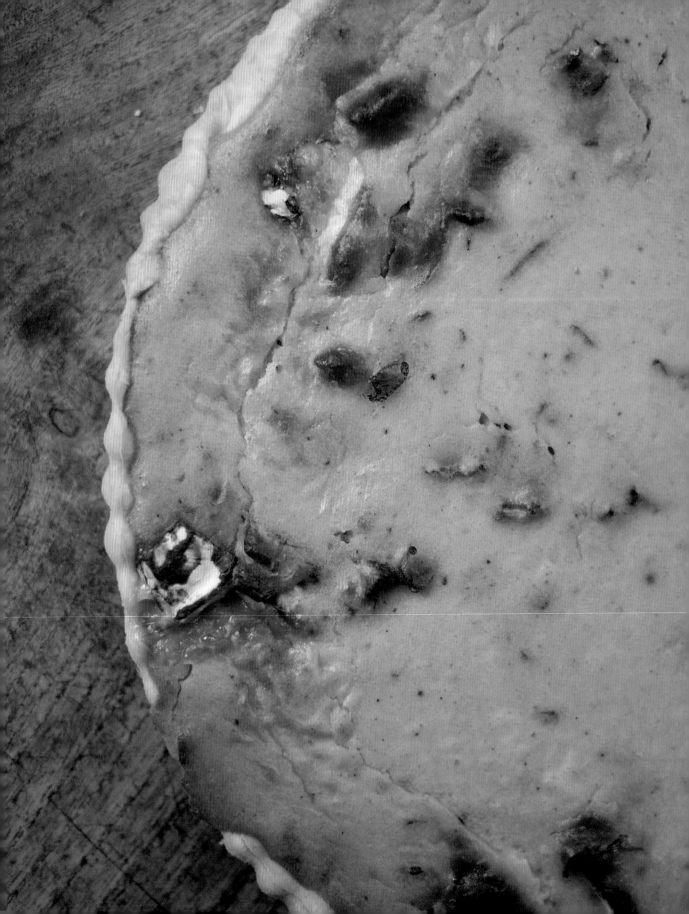

Murray's Cheese shop in New York so that the downtown Greenwich villagers should be supplied with their choicest, dream tarts and pies over the holiday. I had to make the classics, the sweet pumpkin pie and pecan pie, to which I added my bitter chocolate tart and my cheddar and onion pie made with unpasteurised farmhouse English Cheddar. The sweetness and spice of pumpkin pie is really not to my taste, but suppose I could conjure up a savoury alternative, would the locals buy it?

Murray's crottin de Chavignol seemed to have the desired sharpness and shardiness and, as it is aged and goaty, also pungence and unmeltability. The medicinal sage is a *sine qua non* with pumpkin and squash – surely frazzling it would add crispness too? And the lactic crème fraîche would help to unsweeten the roasted squash.

We sold large and small tarts, exceeding our orders several times over, and this has become my new favourite. Good enough for any occasion.

SPINACH, CROTTIN DE CHAVIGNOL, TOMATO AND PARMESAN TART

SERVES 6–8

1 x 23cm/9in shortcrust pastry tart case, made with 170g/6oz flour to 85g/3oz butter (see pages 116 and 197)

3 large handfuls of spinach, as big a fist of leaves from the bag or garden as you can manage

3–4 tbsp double cream

2 eggs and 2 egg yolks

sea salt, black pepper and a smidgen of nutmeg

2 heaped tbsp crème fraîche

1 crottin de Chavignol

2 large tomatoes, sliced and cored

enough freshly grated Parmesan to gratinée the top, about 3–4 tbsp

Make the pastry, refrigerate it and bake it blind (see page 197), letting it dry out for 5 minutes before you spill the filling ingredients into its midst.

Preheat the oven to 200°C/400°F/gas 6. Meanwhile, wash the spinach and put it in a pan with only the residual washing water. Stir briskly over a high heat to stop it sticking and burning – for just long enough for it to wilt and collapse. Blitz in a food processor with the cream, but just to the point where the spinach is in large, speckledy blobs, not tiny tweedy ones that are purée rather than texture. It's most important to stop that uniform smoothness that tarts can have if you're not careful!

Now beat in the eggs and egg yolks and season, not too much salt because of the crottin. Add a suspicion of nutmeg, spinach's best friend. Whisk in the crème fraîche. Cover the bottom of the tart case which you've just removed from the oven with the shards of crottin, then pour over the green mixture. Turn the oven down to 175°C/350°F/gas 4 and cook the tart for 15 minutes. Take it out of the oven and carefully plop the slices of tomato on the semi-set greenery. Strew over a generous handful of Parmesan to cover the top, while leaving some of the tomato bare enough to peak through. Continue to cook until the Parmesan has obviously gone from golden to bronzed, crusted gratin and the whole is puffed up and just this side of too much wobble. Leave the tart on a rack for at least 15 minutes to allow the air to circulate beneath it before you venture to cut and eat it.

The butternut squash and crottin de Chavignol tart (see page 116) worked so well, I wanted to try other flavours and textures with the dry, salt, crumbly goat's cheese. It has so intense a flavour it can stand up to the iron of spinach, the salt strength of Parmesan and the acidity of the soft, fruity tomato. This is an unusual and delicious tart, puffed up until greenly golden and bubbling and crusted with a gratin of Parmesan. Any aged goat's crottin would work well, the Chavignol is one I find particularly splendiferous.

MASCARPONE, THYME AND SMOKED BACON TART

SERVES 6–8

1 x 23cm/9in shortcrust pastry tart case, made
with 170g/6oz flour to 85g/3 oz butter (see pages
116 and 197)

7 or 8 smoked streaky rashers, the rind removed
with scissors

200g/7fl oz mascarpone

200g/7fl oz crème fraîche

2 eggs and 2 egg yolks

sea salt and a good scrunch of coarsely ground
black pepper, you may like to do this in a mortar

2 tbsp fresh thyme leaves stripped from the stems

1–2 tbsp bacon fat

Preheat the oven to 200°C/400°F/gas 6. Make the pastry and bake it blind (see page 197).
Meanwhile, lay the bacon rashers (I favour Swaddles organic, smoked without nitrates) on the
bottom of a hot frying pan and cook them until they have browned and crisped on both sides.
If you need to get rid of some of the fat at half time to prevent excess smoking and spitting, pour
it into another pan and use it to fry the thyme leaves for a minute.

Drain the rashers on kitchen paper and crumble 3 of them into chunky shards to place on the
bottom of the baked and dried-out tart case.

Whisk the mascarpone and crème fraîche together with the eggs, egg yolks and seasoning,
then stir in the briefly fried thyme and bacon fat. A minute should give you the release of thyme
oil you need for its heavenly scent to perfume the tart. Pour this mixture over the tart case and
turn the oven down to 175°C/350°F/gas 4. Cook for 15 minutes before gently placing the long,
remaining crisped rashers over the surface. They should not sink, but if they begin to, try again
in 5 minutes. Continue to bake the tart until puffed up, brown and tremblingly but not dangerously
set. Wait 15 minutes with the tart on a rack before you serve it.

This three-note tart is raised to the heavens by a couple
of minor tweaks. The thyme is chopped and briefly fried
in bacon fat to release its own inimitable oiled scent and
the smoked streaky rashers are crisped to shatter point.
Both are crumbled into the tart and also left lying longly
and leanly on its summit at cross purposes, as it were, to
snap saltily when you bite into the softness below. Thyme
is under used and a wonderful herb with all things porky.

CLASSIC CAKES

3

AUNTIE FEI'S SOUR CREAM COFFEE CAKE

Cake batter
55g/2oz butter
340g/12oz unrefined caster sugar
4 eggs
225/8oz flour
½ tsp bicarbonate of soda
1½ tsp baking powder
200ml/7fl oz sour cream
1 tsp vanilla extract

Filling
110g/4oz cream cheese
1 egg
1 tbsp sugar

30g/1oz dried cranberries or 1 cooking apple,
   peeled and diced
30g/1oz walnuts, toasted and roughly chopped

Topping
110g/4oz flour
110g/4oz sugar
1 tsp salt
1½ tsp ground cinnamon
85g/3oz walnuts, toasted and roughly chopped
30g/1oz melted butter
½ tsp vanilla extract
½ tsp almond extract

Cream the butter and sugar until light and fluffy. Add the eggs one at a time, mixing well between each one. Sift the dry ingredients together and combine the sour cream and vanilla in a separate bowl. Alternately add the sour cream mixture and dry ingredients to the butter and sugar in three phases, combining well each time.

For the filling, beat together the cream cheese, eggs and sugar until smooth. To make the topping, mix together the flour, sugar, salt, cinnamon and walnuts. Add the butter and extracts and stir.

To assemble the cake, pour half the cake batter into a greased bundt pan and sprinkle with the cranberries or diced apple and the toasted walnuts. Pour the cream cheese mixture evenly over the nuts and berries and cover with the remaining batter. Sprinkle the topping over the whole cake. Bake at 180°C/350°F/gas 4 for 50–55 minutes.

It has taken me until now to realise that in America a coffee cake isn't a coffee cake. It is a cake to eat while you drink coffee, but it has absolutely no coffee in its make-up. I can't say I was exactly disappointed when I discovered this, though I felt a little cheated, and not a trifle stupid about the fact that I had never quite brought myself to ask why I could not detect even the subtlest aroma of caffeine in any breakfast cake I had ever chomped in America. It seemed so contrary, so perverse, when I found out. Imagine being given strawberry ice cream that was in fact just vanilla ice cream, but seen as a perfect partner to a luscious ripe strawberry? Wouldn't your saliva glands already be responding in a strawberryish way? Or think of a lemon tart,

Coffee cake without the coffee. The delectable sour cream coffee cake that Rob would kill for – breakfast time, teatime, any time.

As long as they have a good, strong, fruity flavour, any sort of berries will work well squished between these little circles of shortcake with cream. Use strawberries, raspberries, blueberries or blackcurrants, or a mixture of any or all of them. This is a perfect impromptu summer recipe that can be put together swiftly. The doughy scones are cooked in 15 minutes and served warm, making the fruit go further and turning it into a substantial pudding.

BLUEBERRY SHORTCAKES

SERVES 3

225g/8oz blueberries, sharp well-flavoured ones like 'Herbert'
sugar
240ml/8fl oz double jersey cream

Shortcake
225g/8oz flour
1½ tbsp unrefined granulated sugar
a pinch of salt
2½ level tsp baking powder
140g/5oz unsalted butter
150ml/5fl oz double Jersey cream

Keep the berries whole if they are small, or halve them. Put them in a bowl and sprinkle them with a little sugar to get the juices going. Whip the cream so that it holds softly and put it in a bowl in the fridge to chill.

Preheat the oven to 230°C/450°F/gas 8. Sift together the dry ingredients for the shortcakes and rub in half the butter, just as you would for shortbread. Mix to a soft dough with the cream, then knead like bread for a minute. Roll out on a floured board, keeping the dough thick enough to cut out six 7.5cm/3in rounds with a scone cutter.

Grease a baking sheet and put three of the rounds on it. Melt a little of the remaining butter and brush it over the circles then put the last three rounds on top. Bake for 10–15 minutes, but check at 10; you want golden scones, not burnt and brown. Separate the double rounds and put the sugared berries on half of them, with or without some whipped cream. Cover with the top decks and more berries and cream.

MARMALADE LAYER CAKE

140g/5oz bitter, fine-cut marmalade (and the rest of the 450g/1lb jar)
250ml/8fl oz double cream, Jersey if possible
140g/5oz plain flour
1 tsp baking powder

2 large, organic eggs
110g/4oz unrefined vanilla caster sugar, plus an extra tbsp for whipping
1 tbsp milk
1 tsp vanilla extract

Preheat the oven to 180°C/350°F/gas 4. Butter and lightly flour two 20cm/8in round cake tins and put a disc of greaseproof or bakewell paper in the base of each. Warm 140g/5oz of marmalade over a low heat in half the cream and keep it warm while you mix the cake.

In a clean bowl, beat the eggs with the sugar until thick and creamy, using an electric whisk or a KitchenAid. Lightly beat in the cream and marmalade mixture, then sift over the flour and baking powder. Fold the flour and batter together quickly and evenly using the spatula, so that the mix does not deflate. Divide it evenly between the tins and bake for 20–25 minutes or until risen and barely firm. Remove from the oven and leave to cool in the tins on a rack. If you prefer, make one larger sponge and adjust the cooking time accordingly; start testing by piercing with a skewer after 25 minutes and cook longer if you need to. Test again every 5 minutes.

Remove the cakes from the tins and peel off the paper. Whip the remaining half of the cream with the milk, vanilla and the tablespoon of sugar until fluffy, then spread half on top of each layer. Stack one on the other as evenly as you can and serve. I like to take Dan's recipe a stage further and fold a large tablespoon of marmalade into the cream. It gives it bitterness and texture, assuaging the richness of the cream a little. I also like to add a heaped tablespoon of marmalade to the top of the sponge once it has cooled – you may need to gently warm it first. (These last two tablespoons of marmalade should finish the pot.) Let this cool before adding the whipped marmalade cream topping. Great served with a blood orange salad.

I have long been a fan of bread guru Dan Lepard and his books and articles. A few months ago, I found a newspaper cutting with this cake recipe and knew its bitter orange marmalade filling would be worth trying. I always have spare jars of marmalade for the lean months, after making a truckload of organic Seville orange marmalade in late January. Dan advises that the only tricky part of this cake is folding the flour into the beaten eggs, which has to be done quickly and with a very light hand to keep the cake airy. Other than that, the only real challenge, if you don't make your own marmalade, is to find one bitter enough and gloopy enough; commercial marmalade tends to be over-sweet and have over-set gel.

I make my version of this cake in a single layer and cook the sponge a little longer. I also change the topping, making it in two different ways as you will see.

I often go to the shop Books For Cooks in Notting Hill, London, and their small café at the back. Every so often they bring out a small volume of recipes from their staff of cooks who cook in the café and from some of their favourite food writers. I have always made fruit muffins with crumble tops and they have expanded the form to this cake, which could be made with any seasonal fruit, such as cranberry, blackcurrant, blackberry and apple, peach, pear or plum. I use dried ginger root in my version as the intensity of its flavour works so well with rhubarb, but if you can't get it, the ground stuff will do, and I prefer the taste of muscovado to granulated in my crumble top.

RHUBARB AND GINGER CRUMBLE CAKE

SERVES 8

Crumble
110g/4oz plain flour
4 tbsp light muscovado sugar
85g/3oz unsalted butter

Fruit
750g/1lb 10oz rhubarb cut into 1cm/½in chunks
1 tbsp unrefined vanilla caster sugar, or to taste
1 tsp ground dried ginger root

Cake
170g/6oz softened, unsalted butter
170g/6oz unrefined vanilla caster sugar
3 organic eggs, beaten
170g/6oz plain flour
2 tsp baking powder
1 tbsp milk

Preheat the oven to 190°C/375°F/gas 5. Butter a 25cm/10in springform cake tin and line the base with baking parchment. Pulse all the crumble ingredients together briefly until they cohere in a crumbly way. Toss the chopped rhubarb with the sugar and spice in a bowl. You may like to add a little more sugar.

Beat the butter and sugar for the cake together with an electric beater or in a KitchenAid until they are pale and fluffy. Beat in the eggs, a little at a time, sprinkling in a tablespoon of sifted flour when you have added about half the beaten egg to stop it curdling. Sift in the rest of the flour and baking powder and fold in gently but thoroughly. Fold in the milk.

Scrape the cake mixture into the cake tin, followed by the rhubarb and sprinkle the crumble on top. Bake for about an hour. The crumble should be golden and crunchy and the rhubarb cooked through by then. Place on a rack and cool for 15 minutes, then either release the spring and unmould the cake to serve warm with cream, preferably clotted, or leave until cold to turn out and eat for tea.

BLONDIES, DATE AND WALNUT BROWNIES

55g/2oz unsalted butter
200g/7oz light muscovado sugar
1 organic egg, beaten
100g/3½oz flour
1 level tsp baking powder

½ tsp sea salt
scraped-out seeds of 1 vanilla pod
55g/2oz pitted dates
55g/2oz walnuts

Preheat the oven to 180°C/350°F/gas 4. Melt the butter in a pan over a low heat and the moment it is liquid, add the light muscovado sugar. Stir it in, still over a gentle heat, only to the point at which the sugar, too, is melted. If you take it too far to bubbling toffee, it will harden instead of staying liquid.

Remove the pan from the heat and whisk in the egg while the mixture is still warm. Sift the flour, baking powder and salt into the pan and scrape in the vanilla seeds. Cut the dates into good-sized nuggets and break the walnuts likewise, adding them both to the mixture.

Line a shallow baking tin, 18cm/7in, or a small loaf tin, with greased bakewell paper so that it covers two of the sides and make sure you grease the other two sides thoroughly. Pour the mixture into the tin. Bake for around 25 minutes, but insert a skewer at 20 minutes and see if it comes out clean. Place the tin on a rack for 10 minutes before cutting the brownies into rectangles and cooling them on the rack.

Is there ever a good reason not to make the most mallowy and moist of bitter chocolate brownies, preferably with a dark hint of coffee and roasted hazelnuts atop or walnuts betwixt? The answer is yes. There is an alternative, and now I have found it I am every bit as hooked on it as on the originals. I am now victim to these date and walnut brownies, also known as blondies. They are an American alternative with the squidgiest, gookiest middles and the thinnest of crisp, fragile-to-the-touch sugared tops hiding the sweet nuggets of date and squirls of chopped walnuts. It is impossible to eat only one. The fragrant note of the muscovado and the way the slice pulls apart in your hand with sticky resistance are compulsive. Beware.

A streusel is just a crumble-topped cake, Austrian in origin, with the crumble providing a good crunch to an otherwise plain, spongy-textured cake. I think this is delicious eaten warm with clotted cream, but you could also eat it American coffee-cake style, with your coffee. It works as well with blackcurrants, which also have a zingy, sharp acidity like the cranberry. I have adapted this from the wonderful *Fruit Book* that Jane Grigson published in 1982.

CRANBERRY STREUSEL CAKE

Cake
1 large organic egg
55g/2oz softened unsalted butter
85g/3oz demerara sugar
85g/3oz self-raising flour
½ level tsp baking powder
2 tbsp cranberry or freshly squeezed orange juice

Topping
85g/3oz cranberries, left whole
85g/3oz demerara sugar
85g/3oz plain flour
55g/2oz unsalted butter
1 tsp cinnamon, ground in a mortar

Preheat the oven to 180°C/350°F/gas 4. Tip all the ingredients for the cake into a KitchenAid or electric mixer and beat well until smooth, or mix by hand. Line the sides and the base of an 18cm/7in square tin or a round springform tin with greaseproof or bakewell paper and grease everything well. Pour in the mixture and flatten it down level with a palate knife. Throw the cranberries over the mixture in an even layer.

Mix the remaining topping ingredients together by hand or in a food processor as you would for a crumble. Pour the mixture over the cranberries, making sure it is in an even layer with the side of a sharp knife.

Bake in the centre of the oven for about 50 minutes or until cooked. Test with a long skewer poked right down through the crumble into the cake – it should come out clean. Cool in the cake tin on top of a rack for 10 minutes to allow the air to circulate, then lift the cake out of the tin with the ends of the bakewell paper. Cool to warm on the rack before serving if it is for a pudding, or leave to cool completely.

UPSIDE-DOWN PEAR AND SPICE CAKE

SERVES 8

4 firm, ripe pears
lemon juice
110g/4oz unsalted butter
340g/12oz light muscovado sugar

Cake
110g/4oz unsalted softened butter
225g/8oz unrefined vanilla caster sugar
2 organic eggs
170g/6oz self-raising flour
2 tsp cinnamon, pounded to powder in a mortar
1 tsp grated dried ginger root or ground ginger
60ml/2fl oz milk

Preheat the oven to 190°C/375°F/gas 5. Grease a 23–25cm/9–10in springform tin. Peel the pears, cut into quarters and rub with fresh lemon juice.

To make the toffeed base of the cake, gently melt the butter with the sugar in a pan. When the sugar has dissolved, turn up the heat and add the quarters of pear, turning them in the syrup for about 4 minutes. Pour the sticky syrup into the base of the tin and arrange the pears in spokes, bulbous ends at the edge of the tin.

Put all the cake ingredients into a KitchenAid or food mixer and beat well until they are light and smooth and well mixed. Scrape the mixture over the pears and smooth it down level with a palette knife. Bake in the middle of the oven for about an hour, or until a skewer inserted into the middle comes out clean. Cool on a rack for 10 minutes so that the cake can shrink from the sides a little, then invert onto a large plate and serve warm with a dollop of clotted cream.

The upside-down cake is one of those culinary thrills that childhood memory accords classic status. It should, like chocolate mousse, flapjacks, petticoat tails or treacle tart, remain part of our kitchen lore and landscape, and be revisited and re-established, particularly for children. Naked fruit on top of a cake, rather than lurking inside it or under it, is somehow far more exciting and stimulating to the taste buds. This is, in its way, our English version of the French classic, tarte tatin.

A CLASSIC FINISH

4

FRUITS OF THE FOREST AND PORT JELLY

1 x 500g/1lb 2oz bag frozen fruits of the forest, organic if possible
110g/4oz unrefined vanilla caster sugar
300ml/10fl oz water

4 leaves gelatine, or consult the packet to check gelatine to liquid ratio
2 tbsp Rock's organic blackcurrant cordial
150ml/5fl oz port

Pour the frozen fruits directly into a large pan with the sugar and water. Bring to the boil and gently simmer for 10 minutes with the lid on. Place a large nylon sieve over a bowl and tip the contents of the pan straight into it, leaving the juices to drip as you would for a potted jelly. Don't press the fruit down to extract more juice unless you don't mind a cloudy jelly. I prefer mine as clear and dark as the night sky! Throw away the contents of the sieve; they have done their work.

Soak the gelatine leaves in a shallow saucer of water for 5 minutes, turning them over at half time. When the gelatine is softened all over, put it into the drained juice in a pan, add the port and blackcurrant cordial and warm everything through together very gently.

Pour the jelly into little plastic pudding basins you can turn out, or into a large jelly mould or glass bowl, or individual ramekins to set. As long as there is a little cold water shaken into whatever option you choose, the jelly will set and turn out. It will need at least 8 hours or overnight, so this is a great pudding to get ahead with. Jelly and ice cream, that standard children's party duo, is still delicious for grown-ups if home-made with the best ingredients. Try this one with a cassis sorbet or a raw blackcurrant ice cream, or even with a home-made vanilla ice cream, seamed through with a ripple of redcurrant or raspberry curd (see page 154).

Port is very good with a number of fruits: figs, raspberries, blackcurrants, blueberries and blackberries, the sort of fruits I crave in midwinter even though I know I can't have them. I am not a great freezer of fruit. There are a few Victoria plums from my tree in plentiful years, apples laid down in the barn, but never enough berries to last beyond the summer. They are all turned into puddings or jams and jellies the moment they're picked. Uncharacteristically though, I sometimes make this jelly in winter, buying a bag of frozen fruits of the forest and conjuring up the taste of a warm July day in a not-so-warm midwinter cold snap. In the summer, use whatever combination of berries you can lay your hands on: currants (red, white or black), loganberries, raspberries, blueberries, blackberries, white waxy cherries or deep red cherries. Just don't use strawberries – when cooked they lose both their magical flavour and their texture, and turn to pink squish.

PINEAPPLE AND YOGHURT FOOL

SERVES 6

1 large, ripe pineapple, about 1kg/2¼lb
1 lime
2 tbsp unrefined vanilla caster sugar

1 tbsp Kirsch
400ml/14fl oz thick live yoghurt (cow's, sheep's
  or Greek)

Cut the ends off the pineapple and cut down, removing the skin from top to bottom. Make sure you remove all the brown snodgels as you go. Remove the tough central core, too, as you cut the fruit into wedges from top to bottom. Cut the wedges into smaller chunks and blitz in a food processor until turned to pulp but still retaining some texture, rather than being a smooth purée.

   Scrape the pineapple into a bowl and grate the zest of the lime over it. Squeeze over the juice of the lime and sprinkle on the sugar and Kirsch. Cover and refrigerate for six hours. Stir the yoghurt into the pineapple pulp and spoon the fool into glasses or a large glass bowl. You may decorate with mint leaves if you like, though I find their ubiquity in restaurants puddings a little annoying. A little more lime zest over the top is my preference.

Fruit fools are one of the unparalleled and simple pleasures of the summer season, so I have always tried to extend the pleasure and fast forward it to the winter with prunes, Hunza apricots, a mix of raspberries and cranberries, mangoes. There has always been a problem, though, with one of my favourite exotic fruits, the pineapple. It doesn't translate into fool-hood successfully. I don't know why the mix of pineapple and cream should diminish the singularly luscious, full-throated flavour of the pineapple, but diminish it it does. It is the same with pineapple ice cream, the fruit clamouring for attention but not really able to win through. So I wondered what would happen if I tried to keep its sharpness in place with yoghurt rather than cream, and unbelievably it worked. I am not a great fan of yoghurt fools or ice creams, but for pineapple this is the only way. Lime juice brings out the flavour of the pineapple magically, as it does with mangoes and melons. Try it and see. Just be sure to make the fool a good six hours before you need it, or the night before.

PEACH AND VANILLA CUSTARD ICE CREAM

MAKES ABOUT 1.2 LITRES/2 PINTS

6 large organic egg yolks
140g/5oz vanilla caster sugar
2 vanilla pods, split down the middle and the seeds
  scooped out with a sharp-pointed teaspoon
500ml/18fl oz Jersey milk

600ml/1 pint double cream, Jersey is best
5 ripe peaches, French or Italian white peaches if
  possible
a spritz of lemon juice

Separate the eggs, putting the whites in one bowl and the yolks in another with the vanilla sugar and the vanilla seeds. Whisk the yolks, sugar and vanilla seeds together until they amalgamate. Slowly heat the milk with the split pods until it reaches scalding point. Pour it straight over the yolk and sugar mixture through a sieve, whisking as you go. Return the mixture to the pan over a very gentle heat and continue to whisk, watching carefully so that no bits of the mixture overheat and scramble at the edges of the pan; the mixture should not get to simmer point. It should take 10–15 minutes, whisking continuously, for the mixture to thicken. Remove the pan from the heat and stir in the double cream. Leave to cool until it is warm rather than hot, stirring every so often so a skin doesn't form on top.

Cut the peaches in half, remove the stones and then cut each half into three. Blitz the peaches to a pulp in the blender and squeeze over a spritz of lemon juice to bring out the flavour. Fold the peach pulp into the custard mixture Churn in an ice-cream machine and finish freezing in the freezer in its pail.

If you are making the ice cream by hand, put the mixture in a sealable plastic container once it has cooled completely and put it in the freezer. Every 30 minutes, remove from the freezer and whisk the ice cream to stop crystals forming and ruining the smooth, velvety texture. When the ice cream has set enough to be difficult to whisk, even in the middle, just leave it in the freezer until it has set completely.

Here is an ice cream where subtlety works. It is particularly good if you have found the best, scented, white peaches with the perfect acid-sweet balance, but we all know how hard this can be.

A fruit curd takes a matter of minutes to make and is really not a technical feat of any seriousness or wizardry. As you stir the fruit, sugar, butter and eggs, the cohesion happens as slowly and steadily as a custard. Suddenly you have it, that gel-like buttery-sharp gloopiness that's about as spoon-lickingly good as you can imagine. And there is no reason to stick to lemon curd. Make this ice cream with redcurrant, blackcurrant or raspberry curd. The quantities and method are the same for all three.

REDCURRANT CURD ICE CREAM

SERVES 6–8

Redcurrant curd
450g/1lb redcurrants, stripped from their stems
  with the tines of a fork
2 large organic eggs and 3 extra organic egg yolks
110g/4oz unrefined vanilla caster sugar
110g/4oz unsalted butter
Vanilla ice cream (see page 153)

Throw the redcurrants into a blender and blitz them thoroughly. Pass them through a nylon sieve into a bowl, pressing as rigorously as your wrist and wooden spoon allow. In a separate bowl, beat together the eggs, extra yolks and the sugar.

I make my curds in an enormous Le Creuset enamel-bottomed pan; the large surface area makes the curd set quicker. Melt the butter in the pan over a very gentle heat, then stir in the egg and sugar mixture and the sieved fruit. Whisk continuously over a low heat until the whole mixture comes together, between 5 and 10 minutes later. Remove from the heat – the idea is to heat rather than cook the fruit, which would then lose some of its raw flavour and its taste. Pour the curd into a bowl and leave to cool. You may cover it with clingfilm and leave it in the fridge for several days or use it as soon as it is cool.

Make half the amount of vanilla ice cream from the recipe on page 153 or make the full amount and add a different curd to the second half or keep it plain. When you have churned your ice cream to soft-set, scrape it into a container and cut streaks of curd into it with a spoon until you have a lovely rippled ice cream. Clip the lid on and continue to freeze in the freezer.

A gorgeous, crimson-curded, redcurrant-veined vanilla ice cream that will pucker and please all good taste buds.

There is something lethally, sexily appealing about this ice cream. The figs' black-skinned, secret, scarlet interiors are reduced to seedy pulpiness and frozen with a lick of port, a spritz of lemon and a little milk. No custard, no whisking, no critical processes at all – this is a hands-off, make-it-easy ice that is as delicious as it is simple to make. I love its amber-red beauty and the seeded crunchiness that just nudges the ice away from total creaminess. The flavour is delicately fleeting, not strident, not imposing, so taste the mixture after you have added the first two measures of port and decide just how far in the background you wish it to remain. Bear in mind that the port flavour will be more evanescent post freezing, so if you still think you need a touch more, pour in the final tablespoon.

FIG ICE CREAM

SERVES 6
450g/1lb black figs, peeled
2–3 tbsp port
110g/4oz unrefined vanilla caster sugar

200ml/7fl oz Jersey or other rich, full cream milk
juice of half an organic lemon

Throw the figs into the blender and blend them until creamy. Add the port, 2 tablespoons to begin with, sugar, milk and juice and blend to smoothness again. Taste and add the third spoonful of port if you feel it is needed. Churn in an ice-cream machine or put in a sealed plastic container and stir every 30 minutes until just set to prevent crystals forming.

PEAR AND GINGERBREAD AND BUTTER PUDDING

SERVES 8

Gingerbread

110g/4oz butter

55g/2oz molasses sugar

55g/2oz demerara sugar

2 eggs

two-thirds of a 450g/1lb jar blackstrap molasses (Meridian make a good one you can buy in healthfood shops)

225g/8oz plain flour

1 tsp grated dried ginger root or powder if you can't get it

5 balls of stem ginger and 2 tbsp of the syrup

2 tbsp milk

scant ½ tsp bicarbonate of soda

Custard

300ml/10fl oz Jersey milk

300ml/10fl oz double cream

1 vanilla pod, split and seeds scraped out

3 eggs

110g/4oz vanilla caster sugar

3 tbsp ginger syrup

To finish

4 firm but ripe Conference pears

juice of a lemon

softened butter to spread on the gingerbread

2 balls of stem ginger, chopped into small dice

First make your gingerbread. Preheat the oven to 170°C/325°F/gas 3. Grease and flour a 18cm/7in loaf tin. Cream the butter and sugars thoroughly, then mix in the eggs one at a time, followed by the blackstrap molasses. Add the dry ginger root with the sifted flour, finely chopped stem ginger and syrup to the cake mixture. Warm the milk slightly and stir it into the bicarb until dissolved, then add to the mixture and fold in. Pour the mixture into the loaf tin and bake for about 1½ hours. Check with a skewer. I favour a sticky, gooey cake, slightly sunken in the middle, so when you turn it out to cool on a rack, it looks like a depressed, blackened brick. When cool, wrap it up in greaseproof paper and foil; it keeps very well for a few days.

To make the custard, scald the milk with the cream, scooped-out vanilla seeds and split pod in a pan. Remove from the heat, cover with a lid and let it infuse for 20 minutes. Whisk the eggs and sugar together thoroughly, then add the milk and cream mixture without the pod and whisk it all together with the ginger syrup.

Preheat the oven to 180°C/350°F/gas 4. Peel the pears and slice vertically down through each pear to make slices 2cm/1¾in thick. Squeeze over some lemon juice to prevent the slices discolouring. Cut the gingerbread into thickish slices and butter them. Place the first layer of gingerbread in the bottom of a gratin or pudding dish and top the layer with slices of pear, then sprinkle some stem ginger dice over them. Add the second layer of buttered gingerbread. Strain the custard mixture over the top. Place the dish in a roasting tin and pour in boiling water to half way up the sides. Put the tin in the oven on the middle shelf and cook the pudding for about 30 minutes or until the custard has just set. Remove and serve warm with clotted cream.

This is a dish that my taste buds conjured up and could imagine the taste of way before I got down to cooking it. Once you have a certain level of experience and knowledge of cooking, you will find that you can taste in your head, well before cooking it, just how a dish ought to turn out. Does that

diminish the thrill of the new? Not an iota; in a sense it enhances it, as the guessing and imagining are finally backed up by the sight and smell and taste of something that has been brewing in the brain until the right time comes along to cook it. We all know how wonderful a truly sticky, black slab of home-made gingerbread is, the sort that sinks like a depressed brick when it's cooked. We know how well ginger goes with pears. Add a home-made custard to the equation and you have strong, molasses-flavoured seams of treacly gingerbread sandwiched with strata of juicy firm pears, unctuous custard and sweet stem ginger.

SLOW-ROASTED PEARS AND QUINCES IN RED WINE AND SPICES

SERVES 8

8 firm, ripe pears, Williams or red Williams
2 quinces
half a lemon
300ml/10fl oz pint red wine
1 cinnamon stick

juice of 2 clementines, satsumas, or a sweet orange
1 star anise
2–3 tbsp light muscovado sugar

Peel the pears, retaining their stalks, and rub them with a cut lemon to prevent discolouring. Peel the quinces, quarter them and remove the cores very carefully; they are rock-like uncooked. Rub with lemon juice. Cut the quince into smallish cubes.

While you are doing this, heat the wine with the cinnamon and let it boil and reduce by almost a half, adding the clementine juice at the end. Stand the pears snugly in a heavy-bottomed pot, add the cubes of quince, then pour over the boiling wine. Taste. If the cinnamon has left its mark, remove it. If not, leave it in while the pears begin to cook. Add the star anise and then throw in 2–3 tablespoons of muscovado sugar. The quinces will need it more than the pears.

Cut out a circle of greaseproof to fit inside the pan. Return to boiling point, press the circle of paper down to fit over the fruit and cover with the lid. Cook slowly, checking after 30 minutes and turning the pears to redden them all over. They may take 1–1½ hours at this temperature, but check every 20 minutes after the first half hour that the pears are easily poked through with a skewer but not limp and soft. Likewise the quince. Remove the cinnamon at any stage if you think the liquor is spiced enough. Good with clotted or thin cream.

With their graininess and their jewel-like, deep-garnet glow once they have been cooked in red wine, both these pear-shaped fruits are at once sumptuous and plain spoken. This is good hot, warm or chilled, perhaps with a home-made vanilla, nutmeg, cinnamon or clove ice cream. By cooking the cubes of quince first in the reduced, ruby wine and juice, their flavour will permeate the syrup and, although they take far longer than pears to soften, there will be no danger of them remaining bullet-like.

MIDDLE EASTERN WINTER FRUIT SALAD

SERVES 6–8

2 dozen or so organic dried, unsulphured apricots
juice of 8 or so clementines, or enough oranges,
  to cover the apricots when soaking
4 organic oranges
12–15 medjool dates, pitted and halved

1 pomegranate
1 tbsp orange flower water
1–2 passion fruit
peel of 1 organic orange and 1 organic lemon

Put the unsulphured apricots in a bowl and pour over the freshly squeezed clementine or orange juice to cover. Leave for at least 6 hours.

Gently simmer the apricots in the juice in a covered pan until tender right through when pierced with a skewer. Leave to cool.

Cut off the ends of the oranges with a sharp knife. Stand each one on its end and work the knife down from top to bottom, cutting off the peel all the way around and making sure any extra bits of pith are removed. Now insert the knife blade just inside a peg on one side and cut into the middle. Do the same with the other side of the peg so the segment comes out with no skin. Segment two of the four oranges in this way. The other two should be peeled as before, removing all the pith as well as the skin, then sliced into thin circles.

Put the orange pegs and circles in the bowl with the apricots and their juice and throw in the dates. Halve the pomegranate and squeeze in a few seeds, then squeeze the juice from both halves in a squeezer and add it to the bowl. Add the orange flower water. Halve one passion fruit and sieve the juice without the seeds into the fruit salad. Taste for sharpness; you may need two. Remove the peel from an orange and a lemon with a potato peeler and slice it into fine matchstick strips. There should be no pith on the underside. In a small pan, boil a little water and simmer the strips for a couple of minutes. Drain and add them to the fruit salad before serving.

This combination of fresh and dried fruit, with exotic passion fruit and pomegranate juice added to the clementine and orange flower water syrup, is a brilliantly festive, scented dish, which involves almost no effort. The organic fresh medjool dates are the ones to use, not the horribly over-sweetened ones in boxes or the dried version. The sharp apricots and the tang of the oranges keep the dates from being too cloyingly sweet. Allow six hours or more for the apricots to plump up in the juice before you cook them. I don't add sugar to the apricots, but you may like to add a little muscovado as they cook if you have a particularly sweet tooth. Keep a steady hand with the orange flower water, or the dish will remind you of bubble bath.

The back lot! All cooks need clean clothes to start spilling food over once they're back at the stove. My problem is I always forget to take things off the line, even when the photographer is around.

I have always loved the scent of cinnamon and apple, the combination of autumnal spiciness with a whiff of the souk. I find this brittle, snappable, rust-coloured stick that unfurls like a fat cigar works as well with savoury as with sweet things if you don't use it recklessly. Cinnamon is also a natural with plums and so is whiskey. The almost tobaccoey, dry tones of the Irish stuff are perfect with the sharp acidity of the fruit. If it is Victoria plum time, late August or early September, look no further. If the plums have been flown in later in the year from sunnier climes, make sure they are not just tasteless bullets. Deep, dark, crimson or purpley black orbs with flavour, a good sweet/acid balance and enough firmness of flesh so they don't collapse the minute they hit the heat are what you want.

WHISKIED PLUM AND MUSCOVADO BROWN BETTY

SERVES 4–6

Fruit
55g/2oz unsalted butter
14–18 plums, halved and stoned
2 tbsp demerara sugar
2 tbsp dark muscovado sugar
2 tbsp Irish whiskey

Topping
55g/2oz unsalted butter
140g/5oz bread, wholemeal, white or granary, torn
  to crumbs and shards by hand
55g/2oz light muscovado sugar
2 tsp cinnamon, ground from a cinnamon stick
  in a mortar with 1 tsp allspice

Melt 55g/2oz of butter in a large heavy-bottomed frying pan and when it begins to foam, add the plums in a single layer, cut side down. Sprinkle the sugars over them and cook gently for about 10 minutes, turning occasionally. Cook until the plums are not resistant when pierced with a knife tip, but don't let them collapse – you want them to hold their shape. Add the whiskey and bubble to amalgamate with the sticky, sugary juices until they form a thick, almost molten-looking goo. Remove from the heat while you make the topping.

Melt the butter for the topping in another frying pan. When it begins to bubble, throw in the breadcrumbs and turn to coat them in butter. Keep cooking the crumbs, remembering to stir them every so often, until they have turned golden and crisp. This takes longer than you would imagine, so be patient and make sure you don't overdo it and turn them black. Once they have crisped, remove them from the heat and stir in the sugar and the spices. Taste and adjust.

Serve the two separately so people can scatter their hot, butter-crisped crumbs over their sticky, whiskied plums. Serve with clotted or pouring cream.

A simple, elegant dish for when you can't be bothered to fuss but need a little something sweet at the end of a meal. The figs can always be served with a good honey or vanilla ice cream.

FIGS IN RED WINE WITH RASPBERRIES

SERVES 4

16 ripe black figs

16 raspberries

a tiny piece of butter for each fig

a handful of light muscovado sugar

red wine

Preheat the oven to 170°C/325°F/gas 3. Cut a cross down, but not right through, each fig so that you can splay them open enough to stuff each one with a raspberry. Place a tiny bit of unsalted butter inside each raspberry. The figs should sit packed tight in a gratin dish so they remain upright. Throw over a handful – a small handful – of muscovado sugar, then pour enough decent red wine over the bottom of the dish to cover its base entirely.

Bake for 20–25 minutes or until the figs are cooked through but holding their shape. Serve hot or warm with cream. A simple, yet exotic dish: the red wine reduces and turns dark and syrupy with the sugar and the marriage of fig and raspberry is a fine one. You could even slip a little burst of raspberry sorbet next to the figs if you are eating them warm rather than hot.

REDCURRANT CURD STEAMED PUDDING

SERVES 6

110g/4oz softened, unsalted butter

170g/6oz unrefined caster sugar

2 organic eggs

zest of 1 organic orange and 1 organic lemon and
  the juice of the orange

110g/4oz self-raising flour

1 tsp baking powder

a little milk to slacken the mixture

285g/10oz redcurrant curd (see page 154) or the
  curd of your choice

Cream the butter and sugar together thoroughly until light and fluffy, then beat in the eggs one at
a time. Add the zests and juice, and sprinkle over the sifted flour and baking powder. You may
need to add a little milk to get the mixture to soft dropping consistency, but don't let it become
too sloppy.

Scrape the redcurrant curd into the greased pudding basin. Spoon the pudding mixture on top
of it – the mixture shouldn't come more than three-quarters of the way up the basin as it will
expand and rise as it steams. Cover with an under-layer of pleated greaseproof and an over-layer
of pleated foil, which both allow room for expansion. Tie string tightly around the foil under the lip
of the bowl, then make a handle with string, winding string around it so that it is strong enough
and short enough to the bowl for you to be able to pick it up easily.

Put the basin on a trivet or piece of folded foil on the bottom of a large, heavy-bottomed pan.
Fill the pan with boiling water to come halfway up the sides of the basin. Put the lid on and keep
the pan at a gentle simmer, topping it up with water if needs be, for about 1½ hours.

Remove the basin from the water and cut off the string. Remove the lid and allow the pudding
a couple of minutes to shrink a little away from the sides. Have a large platter warmed and ready.
Put it upside down over the pudding and turn the pudding out onto it, giving a little shake to
dislodge it as you go. You need a plate with enough depth to contain the moat of curd that will
drown the pudding and slip from its top to its bottom. Serve with clotted or pouring cream.

This is as wonderful a steamed pudding as you can imagine.
As it turns out, the curd plops and dribbles down from its
steaming summit, creating a slalom of bright, sharp, gloopy
sauce. Try it with blackcurrant or redcurrant curd, with
raspberry or divine passion-fruit curd, or go back to basics
and use lemon, lime or orange curd if you prefer. Give tang
to the sweet depths whatever you do; that is what this old-
fashioned classic pudding is all about. Make the curd as for
the ice cream on page 154, then measure out what you need
for this recipe. Use any extra poured over ice cream or for
filling baby tarts.

BLACK FOREST TRIFLE

Kirsch or Cognac
1 x 680g/1½lb jar of stoned morello cherries

Syllabub
240ml/8fl oz white wine, Muscat if possible
6 tbsp Kirsch
zest and juice of an organic lemon
2 tbsp vanilla caster sugar
300ml/10fl oz double cream, Jersey if possible

Sponge
140g/5oz softened butter
85g/3oz vanilla caster sugar
2 eggs, separated

85g/3oz best bitter chocolate, grated
½ tsp salt
200g/7oz self-raising flour
1 tbsp strong fresh coffee
1 tbsp milk

Custard
300ml/10fl oz Jersey milk
300ml/10fl oz double cream, Jersey if possible
2 eggs and 2 egg yolks
1 heaped tbsp cornflour
1 tbsp cocoa powder
vanilla caster sugar to taste

For the syllabub, put the wine, Kirsch, lemon zest and juice in a bowl, cover and leave overnight if possible, or for as long as you have time for. Strain the liquid into a bowl and stir in the sugar until it has completely dissolved. Pour in the cream and begin to beat with a balloon whisk. It seems hard to imagine that the liquid will be taken up and absorbed by the cream to begin with, but it does happen and it doesn't take forever. Keep whisking until the syllabub holds in soft folds. Keep the mixture cool but not very cold or the cream will harden too much.

Make the cake, if you don't have any leftovers to use. Preheat the oven to 180°C/350°F/gas 4. Grease a 20cm/8in tin and line with baking parchment, the paper rising about 2.5cm/1in above the tin. Beat the butter and sugar thoroughly until pale and creamy. Beat the egg yolks and add them to the mixture. Combine the chocolate, salt and flour and stir into the mixture with the coffee and milk. Whisk the whites to stiff peaks, stir the first tablespoon into the cake mixture, then fold in the rest. Stir in a teaspoon of boiling water before scraping the mixture into the tin. Bake for about 45 minutes or until a skewer comes out clean. Cool on a rack.

Cut the sponge into thin sections to fit into the base of a glass bowl or glasses. Sprinkle over a little Kirsch or Cognac. Drain the cherries and sprinkle a layer of them over the cake.

To make the custard, bring the milk and cream to scalding point in a pan. Whisk the eggs and yolks with the sifted cornflour and cocoa powder in a large bowl, then pour over the hot cream and milk whisking as you go. Return to the pan over a medium heat and whisk the custard until it is lump free and thickens discernibly. Add sugar to taste and whisk it in so that it dissolves. Remove from the heat and leave to cool to warm. Give it an occasional whisk in the meanwhile so that a skin doesn't form. Pour over the sponge and cherries. Pile on the syllabub so that the top is billowy rather than flat and decorate as you feel the urge.

This was an improvised pudding, made with the remains of some chocolate cake. Use whatever is your favourite or make the plain sponge above.

This is not about kitsch and retro. It's about the best bitter chocolate sponge, doused in Kirsch and cream, sharp morello cherries and home-made choccy custard

In that short, sharp season before the sap rises and spring is sprung, blood oranges somehow speak of sun, warmth and promise, if only because of their richness of hue. From February until blood oranges peter out in early April, you can make this flourless, almost souffle-like cake with best Marcona almonds and surround it with a moat of sunset-coloured blood orange and mandarin syrup. If the season is over, use ordinary oranges, but do contrast either orange with mandarin juice as this is what makes the syrup unique.

ALMOND CAKE WITH A BLOOD ORANGE AND MANDARIN SYRUP

SERVES 8–10

Cake

8 organic eggs, separated

200g/7oz sugar, half light muscovado, half unrefined caster sugar

grated zest of 2 blood oranges

2 tsp cinnamon

225/8oz best blanched almonds, ground in a food processor until half ground, half nubbly

Syrup

300ml/10fl oz blood orange juice (about 8 oranges)

300ml/10fl oz mandarin juice (about 12 mandarins)

170g/6oz unrefined caster sugar

Cream sauce

300ml/10fl oz double cream, Jersey if possible

1 vanilla pod, seeds scraped out

1–1½ heaped tbsp light muscovado sugar

1–1½ tbsp Cointreau or Grand Marnier (optional)

Preheat the oven to 180°/350°F/gas 4. Beat the egg yolks, sugars, orange zest and cinnamon well in a KitchenAid or with an electric beater. Add the almonds and fold them in. Beat the egg whites to stiff peaks and stir the first tablespoon into the mixture, then fold the rest in lightly. Pour into a greased, floured 25cm/10in springform cake tin and bake for about 40 minutes. Test the cake with a skewer – it might need a further 5 minutes. Put the cake in its tin on a rack to cool.

Meanwhile make the syrup. Squeeze the juice of the blood oranges and mandarins until you have 600ml/1 pint. Pour the juice into a small pan with the caster sugar and bring it slowly to the boil, stirring to dissolve the sugar. Simmer gently until the liquid has reduced by half and is a sticky syrup. Keep it warm enough not to set.

When the cake is tepid, remove it from the tin and place it on a large plate with a lip. Make holes all over it, right through to the bottom, with a meat skewer. Pour the orange syrup into the holes, so that the cake absorbs it. Leave the cake with its sticky pink moat for a few hours, occasionally spooning more syrup over the surface.

Pour the cream into a bowl with the vanilla seeds and sugar and whisk until sloppily firm. Pour in the orange liqueur, 1 tablespoon to start with, and whisk until soft, but holding. Taste and adjust the amount of alcohol if you need to; it should add orange flavour but not be intrusive. Serve in a bowl with the cake.

Top shelf (left to right):

IRELAND — Theodora Fitzgibbon

Claudia Roden — THE BOOK OF JEWISH FOOD

Claudia Roden Arabesque

Recipes from a Spanish Village

PIERRE KOFFMANN — Memories of Gascony — MITCHELL BEAZLEY

RICHARD OLNEY — SIMPLE FRENCH FOOD

Baker & Spice — baking with passion — Lepard/Whittington

SAM & SAM CLARK — Moro THE COOKBOOK

SAM & SAM CLARK — CASA Moro THE SECOND COOKBOOK

Rowley Leigh — No place like home

The Essentials of Classic Italian Cooking — MARCELLA HAZAN

ALASTAIR LITTLE — Keep it simple

ANNA DEL CONTE — Italian Kitchen

The Classic Food of Northern Italy — ANNA DEL CONTE

ELIZABETH DAVID

Bottom shelf (left to right):

The Englishwoman's Kitchen

SIMPLY THE BEST — Tamasin Day-Lewis

Tarts with Tops On — Tamasin Day-Lewis

The Art of the Tart — Tamasin Day-Lewis

Good Tempered Food — Tamasin Day-Lewis

TAMASIN'S KITCHEN BIBLE — TAMASIN DAY-LEWIS

GOOD TEMPERED FOOD — Tamasin Day-Lewis

THE PRAWN COCKTAIL YEARS — SIMON HOPKINSON & LINDSEY BAREHAM

Gammon & Spinach — SIMON HOPKINSON

SIMON HOPKINSON — Roast Chicken and Other Stories Second Helpings

Jane Grigson's Fruit Book — MICHAEL JOSEPH

Jane Grigson's Vegetable Book — MICHAEL JOSEPH

JANE GRIGSON — ENGLISH FOOD

Jane Grigson Fish Cookery

ELIZABETH DAVID

Elizabeth David — French Provincial Cooking

WALNUT, FIG AND ROAST HAZELNUT TREACLE TART

SERVES 8

8 organic dried figs
55g/2oz roast hazelnuts
55g/2oz organic walnuts
110g/4oz softened, unsalted butter
110g/4oz light muscovado sugar
3 organic eggs

170g/6oz golden syrup
1 heaped tbsp blackstrap molasses
grated zest and juice of an organic lemon

Shortcrust pastry
170g/6oz flour
85g/3oz unsalted butter, fridge cold

Make the pastry (see page 197). Preheat the oven to 200°C/400°F/gas 6. Bake the tart case blind for 15 minutes, then remove the beans and foil and put the pastry back in the oven for 5 minutes to dry it out. Dock the base and sides with a fork to prevent them bubbling up.

Trim the stalks from the figs, cut them into small nubbly pieces and put them in a bowl. Chop the roast hazelnuts and walnuts coarsely and add them to the bowl. Cream the softened butter and muscovado sugar thoroughly in a KitchenAid or by hand, making sure the mixture has turned really pale and light. Beat in the eggs one at a time.

Warm the golden syrup and blackstrap molasses gently in a pan until just beginning to turn slightly liquid. Pour them into the creamed mixture, then scrape it all into the bowl of fruit and nuts. Add the juice and zest of a lemon and tip the contents into the baked blind pastry shell. Return it to the oven, turn the temperature down to 180°C/350°F/gas 4 and cook until the tart has set, browned and puffed up a little, but still has a faint quake at its middle. This should take 25–35 minutes. Remove from the oven and cool to warm. Serve with clotted cream or home-made vanilla ice cream (see page 153).

This is so good, so stickily delicious with its roasted nuts and blackly molassesy, zesty undertow, that you almost forget you are no longer in the season of summer or autumnal fruits. However much you are addicted to treacle tart, you will certainly feel that here is something that doesn't just gnaw at your jaw with its saturation sweetness. Here you have different textures, the dense-textured graininess of the figs and the lemony sharpness cutting the blackstrap molasses and muscovado.

I have one tart case that is double the depth of my other ones, so it is good for ice cream tarts, the fig, walnut and hazelnut treacle tart on page 179, deep-dish fruit pies that are not going to ooze too much liquid, and this blueberry tart. There is something about the layers of packed-together-tight blueberries and the sheer quantity of fruit that makes me always want to make it this way – less custard to fruit, more fruit to tart. Allow time to macerate the fruit in the sugar and Kirsch for an hour before you begin so that the berries begin to bleed their black juices. I find a type called 'Herbert' has by far and away the most defined blueberry flavour and best acidity. Many blueberries are too sweet, too squishy and without enough flavour or acidity.

DEEP BLUEBERRY TART

SERVES 6
Shortcrust pastry
170g/6oz flour
85g/3oz unsalted butter, fridge cold

Filling
675g/1½lb blueberries

2 tbsp unrefined granulated sugar
2 tbsp Kirsch
300ml/10fl oz double jersey cream
2 organic eggs and 2 egg yolks
extra tbsp sugar

Preheat the oven to 180°C/350°F/gas 4. Make the pastry (see page 197) and line the tart case. Bake the pastry blind for 15 minutes, then dock the base and sides with a fork and give it another 5 minutes without the foil and beans to dry it out.

Meanwhile, put the blueberries in a deep bowl with the sugar and Kirsch for an hour and turn them gently several times with a spoon so that they begin to weep with juice.

Whisk together the cream, eggs, egg yolks and extra tablespoon of sugar. Put the blueberries into the tart shell with a slotted spoon, then quickly add the sugary, fruity juices to the custard mixture and give it one last whisk. Put the tart on the baking tray on the middle shelf of the oven and pour in the custard from a jug. Turn the oven down to 170°C/325°F/gas 3 and bake until the filling has set to a faint wobble. Check after 30 minutes, but it might take 10–15 minutes longer. Place on a rack and cool in the tart case until warm.

LEMON ICE CREAM TART WITH A GINGER CRUST

SERVES 8

Ginger crust
110g/4oz unsalted butter
400g/13oz ginger biscuits

Ice cream
150ml/5fl oz white wine

2 tbsp dry Marsala or brandy
grated zest and juice of 2 organic lemons
grated zest and juice of 1 organic orange
4 tbsp unrefined vanilla caster sugar
500ml/18fl oz double cream

Line the base of a loose-bottomed tart tin, about 20cm/8in in diameter, with a single piece of greaseproof paper. Melt the butter in a small pan. Crush the biscuits in a food processor or bash them in a plastic bag with a rolling pin – you want a fine powder. Stir the biscuits into the butter. Line the base of the tin with the buttered crumbs, pushing some up the sides as far as you can. It doesn't matter if the edges are rough. Put the crumb-lined tin in the freezer.

Pour the wine into the bowl of a food mixer or a large mixing bowl. Add the Marsala or brandy and the finely grated zest of the lemons and the orange. Squeeze one of the lemons and add the juice. Reserve the orange for later. Add the sugar and cream to the wine and zest mixture and beat slowly until thick. You want the consistency to be soft and thick, so that it lies in soft folds rather than standing in stiff peaks. Scrape the mixture into the crumb-lined tart tin and freeze for at least four hours. Remove from the freezer 15–20 minutes before you intend to serve it. I find it easier to remove the tart from the tin while it is still frozen, running a palette knife around the edge first. Cut the peel from the orange, slice the flesh thinly and serve at the side of each slice. It can be difficult to push the base up and remove the sides for this tart, so if it looks as though it won't work, serve straight from the tart tin.

The raspberry ripple ice cream pie in my book *Tarts With Tops On* is one of the greats of the genre, a pudding that has all the excitement and childish appeal you could hope for when it is turned out onto a plate. This child-like element is something I believe characterises all the best puddings. They are fantasies; they are naughty, wicked, decadent at best, or are certainly described as such by those of us who put words to these thing. They are dishes we drool over and dream about. Savoury things never appeal in quite the same way. Fruit, chocolate, cream, eggs, sugar, nuts; crumbly, crunchy, sticky, sweetness; sharp, creamy, unctuous; these are all ingredients and taste sensations that seduce us to eat and make the things that may not do us good so tempting. But what would life be if we didn't deprive ourselves a little,

RASPBERRY AND VANILLA
CHEESECAKE TART

SERVES 8

Shortcrust pastry
170g/6oz flour
85g/3oz unsalted butter, fridge cold
2 tbsp vanilla caster sugar

Filling
140g/5oz fresh cream cheese, the best, no packet
   equivalent
150ml/5fl oz Jersey double cream
1 heaped tbsp crème fraîche
3 small organic eggs and 2 egg yolks
2 vanilla pods, the seeds scooped out from the
   split pods with a teaspoon
340g/12oz raspberries

Make the shortcrust in the usual way (see page 197), adding 2 tablespoons of vanilla caster sugar to the dry ingredients before you turn the mixture to crumb. Bake blind in a 20cm/8in tin for 15 minutes. Remove the foil and beans, dock the base and sides with the tines of a fork, then return to the oven to dry out for a further 5 minutes.

Meanwhile, assemble and make the filling. Turn the oven down to 180°C/350°F/gas 4. Scrape the cream cheese into a bowl and add the cream, crème fraîche, eggs and yolks, and vanilla to the bowl. Whisk all together to inimitable dense, speckled smoothness. Scatter the raspberries over the base of the baked pastry shell in a single layer, then scrape over the cheesecake mix. Bake for about 45 minutes until golden and trembling set – a mere quake at the middle when nudged in the tin. Cool on a rack.

I am not convinced about the merits of soggy-bottomed cheesecakes, and that, unfortunately, is how the digestive-biscuit-based (or Graham cracker American equivalent) versions often end up. You can have the cream-cheesiest, richest, most lemon-scented, vanilla-rich, egg-lightened cheesecake ruined by the failure of its biscuit bottom. Sometimes it's better just to make a cheesecake with no bottom at all. Or sometimes you may wish to change the mix and make a shortcrust base, as with this distinctively delicious variation. Here the sugar in the shortcrust crispens the pastry so that it is more like a lovely buttery shortcake, and the filling doesn't seem to break its barriers and render it limply damp and soggy!

This is a shocker of a tart, both in colour and culinary terms, and one which will come as a surprise to all who venture into its crimson, spoon-soft depths and its sugar-crisp vanilla-scented base of sweetcrust pastry. No one will be expecting what they find, or that is what I discovered when I first made this vibrant, show-stopper of a tart. It should be served fridge cold so that set curd and crisp pastry vie for attention and contrast. The curd is not stiff enough to stay entirely with the pastry base when you cut into the tart, but don't let that worry you. Once you taste it you will know why. It is quite simply so delicious, the fondant texture so perfect, it doesn't matter. The raspberry curd is made in exactly the same way as the redcurrant curd on page 154.

RASPBERRY CURD TART

SERVES 8

Raspberry curd
450g/1lb raspberries
2 organic eggs and 3 organic egg yolks
110g/4oz unrefined caster sugar
110g/4oz unsalted butter

Sweetcrust pastry
225g/8oz flour
110g/4oz unsalted butter, fridge cold
2 tbsp unrefined organic icing sugar
scraped-out seeds from a vanilla pod
1 organic egg yolk
a little ice-cold water

Sift the flour into a large bowl and add the cubed butter straight from the fridge. Sift in the icing sugar and add the vanilla seeds. Work quickly to a crumb with your fingers. Add the beaten egg and work it in with a tablespoon of cold water. It should cohere without any more water fairly quickly, but if it doesn't, add another tablespoon. Form the pastry into a ball and wrap it in clingfilm. Put it in the fridge to rest for an hour while you make and cool the raspberry curd. Make this exactly as the redcurrant curd on page 154, substituting raspberries for redcurrants.

Grease and line a tart case with the pastry and bake blind for 20 minutes at 200°C/400°F/gas 6. Remove the beans and foil, dock the tart with the tines of a fork and return it to the oven for about 8 minutes to dry and crisp the pastry. It should have begun to colour but not brown. Set aside to cool.

When cold, scrape the curd into the tart shell and place the tart in the fridge overnight or for at least 6 hours. Remove the sides of the tart case and slide the tart off its base onto a large white plate to serve. No cream required here; the intense raspberry and butter richness is all.

A truly classic finish to the book, and one which, like so many others, happened by pure chance. I love coffee in puddings; I love coffee and raspberries together, and these are tastes that came to mind when one night I suddenly had a large dinner to cook and only the fridge and store cupboard at hand. I have always enjoyed a good bavarois, rarely seen either in restaurants or in people's pudding repertoires these days. I pictured something lightly, quakingly set, and remembered the sweet, dark cocoa crust I make with my white chocolate and raspberry tart and how well chocolate goes with coffee and raspberries.

The triumvirate in place, I just followed my instincts, determined to have a strong, grainy hit of freshly brewed coffee and a burst of sharp raspberry contained in a slightly shuddery, creamy bavarois edged with the cocoa crust. It worked first time round and was as good when the flavours had had longer to develop overnight – unusual for pastry, but more usual with a sugary sweet crust which keeps crisper, particularly if its topping isn't liquid when the two are combined. Keep the tart chilled and serve it the next day if it suits you to make it in advance.

COFFEE AND RASPBERRY BAVAROIS TART WITH A COCOA CRUST

SERVES 8

Cocoa crust

170g/6oz flour
2 heaped tsp Green and Black's organic
  cocoa powder
2 tbsp unrefined icing sugar
85g/3oz unsalted butter, fridge cold
1 organic egg yolk
cold water

Bavarois

2 heaped tbsp good, freshly ground coffee
300ml/10fl oz Jersey milk
1 vanilla pod
2 leaves gelatine
4 organic egg yolks
85g/3oz unrefined vanilla caster sugar
300ml/10fl oz double Jersey cream
1 tbsp unrefined icing sugar
a punnet of raspberries, 170g/6oz or so

Make the pastry in the usual way (see page 197): sift the dry ingredients together, then work in the cubes of cold butter or do the whole thing in a food processor. Add the yolk and a tablespoon of water and pulse or work until it coheres. When you roll it out, add a little cocoa to the flour on the board too. Chill, then bake blind for 20–25 minutes before drying out without the beans and foil for a further 5–8 minutes. The pastry needs to be completely cooked for this recipe.

In the meantime, make the bavarois. Put the coffee and milk together in a pan with the split vanilla pod and its seeds scraped out with a teaspoon, and bring slowly to boiling point. Remove from the heat, cover with a lid and leave to infuse for 30 minutes.

Soak the gelatine leaves in a little cold water according to the instructions on the packet while you make the custard. Whisk the egg yolks and sugar together vigorously, then strain the coffee-scented milk into them through a muslin-lined sieve and whisk them together. Heat the custard slowly in the pan and whisk constantly over a low heat until it thickens and coats the proverbial spoon! This should take 10–15 minutes.

Remove from the heat and stir in the squishy gelatine leaves until they have completely dissolved. Let the custard cool to tepid. Whip the cream with a tablespoon of unrefined icing sugar until it holds softly. Fold the cream into the tepid custard, followed by the raspberries, as gently as you can so that they don't break up. Scrape the mixture into the cooled cocoa crust and set it in the fridge to chill until you can keep your hands off it no longer!

CHICKEN STOCK

MAKES ABOUT 1.5 LITRES / 3 PINTS
roast chicken carcass
2 onions, unpeeled and cut in half
4 cloves
2–3 celery sticks, broken in half
2 carrots, chopped

cleaned green tops of leeks and mushroom
  peelings if you have some
bouquet of fresh herbs: parsley, bay, thyme and
  rosemary or any combination of these
a few black peppercorns

Break up the carcass of your roast chicken into large pieces and make sure you save all the bones from people's plates to add. Brown the bones in a roasting tin, then put them in a large, heavy-bottomed pan. Add a couple of onions halved, skins still on for flavour and colour, each half stuck with a clove, and the celery and chopped carrots; chopping the vegetables imparts more flavour than leaving them whole. Throw in some cleaned green tops of leeks if you have them, a few mushroom peelings, a small bouquet of fresh herbs – parsley, bay, thyme and rosemary or any combination of these – and a few black peppercorns. Add the giblets if you haven't already used them for your gravy.

   Cover with cold water, bring slowly to the boil and skim. Simmer, three-quarters covered, for a couple of hours. Don't cook any longer than this – the flavour doesn't improve as I suspect all the goodness has been released by the bones and the vegetables by then. Strain into a bowl and when cold, put in the fridge covered in clingfilm. Take the fat off when you want to use the stock. The fat can be clarified and used as dripping for roast potatoes.

VEGETABLE STOCK

1.2 litres / 2 pints water
240ml/8fl oz dry white wine
2 large carrots, cut into chunks
2 sticks of celery, cut in half
2 medium onions, unpeeled and stuck
  with 2 cloves each
4 shallots

green tops of 3 leeks
2 whole tomatoes
1 bulb of fennel, chopped
a few whole mushrooms or mushroom peelings
a bouquet of fresh thyme, rosemary, parsley
  and bay
1 tbsp white peppercorns

Bring the water and wine to the boil. Add the vegetables and herbs and return to the boil. Skim off any grey froth. When the surface is clear, add the peppercorns: if you add them earlier, you'll skim most of them off. Simmer gently for 40 minutes, then strain.

BEEF OR VEAL STOCK

1kg/2¼lb beef or veal bones
usual stock vegetables: onion, celery, carrot, leek
 tops if you have some, roughly chopped

a bouquet of bay leaves, parsley and thyme tied
 together

Brown the beef bones in a roasting tin, then transfer them to a large pan. Add the vegetables and cover with water. Bring to the boil and skim, then simmer for 2 hours. Strain well.

BASIC BÉCHAMEL SAUCE

600ml/1 pint full-cream milk, Jersey if possible
onion, peeled and stuck with a couple of cloves
bay leaf
55g/2oz unsalted butter

1 heaped tbsp plain flour
nutmeg
sea salt
black pepper

Bring the milk slowly to the boil in a small pan to which you have also added the clove-studded onion and a fresh bay leaf. Then remove the pan from the heat and leave the milk to infuse for 20–30 minutes.

Melt the butter over a gentle heat in a small, heavy-bottomed pan. Just as the butter begins to foam and bubble, throw in a heaped tablespoon of plain flour and stir it gently for a few seconds. Too much flour and you'll get a thick floury base layer to the pan instead of a thin bubbling one; too little and the butter won't amalgamate with the flour, so scatter in a little more. Let this bubble together for a minute or so until it begins to turn a pale biscuit colour, but don't let it darken and begin to burn. Add about half a cup of the milk, which you have heated to hot again, whereupon the mixture will bubble. Whisk it furiously with a small balloon whisk until it suddenly thickens beyond easy whisking. Add more milk and repeat; the sauce will take a little longer to thicken each time you add more milk.

Begin to cook the sauce more slowly while stirring it with a wooden spoon – you should have whisked the lumps out by now – and add more milk as the sauce seems to demand it to keep the texture thick enough but not solid. Cook slowly for 20 minutes, remembering to stir frequently to prevent it sticking to the bottom of the pan and burning, which milk has a tendency to do, and to prevent a skin forming on the surface.

I grate a little nutmeg into the sauce about halfway through the cooking time and season it. When the sauce is cooked, I check the seasoning and adjust it if necessary. Nutmeg is always best when you add a 'suspicion' of it; you don't want the sauce to become a nutmeg sauce.

SHORTCRUST PASTRY

QUANTITY FOR 20–23CM/8–9IN TART TIN

170g/6oz plain white (preferably organic) or
  wholemeal flour

pinch of sea salt
85g/3oz unsalted butter, fridge cold

I sift the flour and a pinch of sea salt into the food processor, then cut the fridge-cold butter into cubes on top of it. Pulse several times for 3-4 seconds a time before adding a tablespoon of cold water through the feed tube. If the paste is still in crumby little bits after a minute or two, add a tablespoon more of water, but remember, the more water you use, the more the pastry will shrink if you bake it blind. The moment it has cohered into a single ball, stop, remove it, wrap it in clingfilm and put it in the fridge for at least 30 minutes.

If you are making pastry by hand, sift the flour into a large bowl with the salt, add the chopped butter, and work as briskly as you can to rub the fat into the flour. Use the tips of your fingers only, rather like running grains of hot sand through your fingers. Add the water bit by bit as above; wrap and chill the pastry.

Now scatter a bit of flour on your work surface, roll your rolling pin in it, dust the palms of your hands, and start rolling. Always roll away from yourself, turning the pastry as you go, and keep the rolling pin and work surface floured to prevent sticking. Once it is rolled out, slip the rolling pin under the pastry, and pick it up, judging where to lie it in the greased tin. Again, never stretch it because it will shrink back. Try to leave at least 30 minutes for the unbaked tart case to commune with the inside of your fridge. Or put it in the fridge the night before you need it.

Baking blind

If you are baking your pastry case blind, preheat the oven to 190–200°C/375–400°F/gas 5–6. Some recipes also tell you to put a baking sheet in the oven to heat up. This can be invaluable if you are using a porcelain or other non-metal tart dish, as the hot baking sheet gives it an initial burst of heat to crisp up the bottom of the pastry. I know that some cooks will be shocked that I could even think of using anything other than metal but, as well as the aesthetic advantage when it comes to serving, china dishes are guaranteed never to discolour the pastry in the way that some metal ones do. If you are using a tart tin with a removable base (my preference, as they are by far the easiest to turn out), placing the tart tin on a baking sheet makes it easier to slide it in and out of the oven.

Tear off a piece of greaseproof paper a little larger than the tart tin and place it over the pastry. Cover the paper with a layer of dried beans; the idea is to prevent the pastry from rising up in the oven. When the pastry is nearly cooked (the timing depends on the rest of the recipe), remove the paper and beans and prick the base of the pastry to let out trapped air that would otherwise bubble up. Return the tart to the oven for 5–10 minutes to dry the pastry base.

INDEX

INDEX

INDEX

INDEX

INDEX

DEDICATION

To the Twelve Pins Club: John and Merci, Michael and Ruth, Susan, Nick, Sal, Rob and all participating children

ACKNOWLEDGMENTS

Thanks in order as always to the usual suspects – Michael Dover, David Rowley, Susan Haynes, Jinny Johnson, Clive Hayball and George Capel – and this time to the new boy who joins peerless food photographer David Loftus. Robert Fairer has shot the day-in-the-life-of pictures with wit, elegance and caught-in-the-moment charm. Right down to the washing line! Thanks to everyone as always for making a beautiful book and for being so good to work with.

First published in Great Britain in 2006
by Weidenfeld & Nicolson
10 9 8 7 6 5 4 3 2 1

Food photography © David Loftus 2006
Styling by Rosie Scott

Location photography © Robert Fairer 2006
Hair and makeup by Natasha Bulstrode
Styling by Lizzy Disney

A CIP catalogue record for this book
is available from the British Library.

ISBN-13: 978 0 297 84428 0
ISBN-10: 0 297 84428 8

Design director David Rowley
Editorial director Susan Haynes
Designed by Clive Hayball
Edited by Jinny Johnson
Proofread by Gwen Rigby
Index by Eliizabeth Wiggans

Printed in Italy

The Orion Publishing Group's policy is to use papers that
are natural, renewable and recyclable products and made
from wood grown in sustainable forests. The logging and
manufacturing processes are expected to conform to the
environmental regulations of the country of origin.

Weidenfeld & Nicolson
The Orion Publishing Group Ltd
Orion House
5 Upper Saint Martin's Lane
London WC2H 9EA
www.orionbooks.co.uk